The Chartered Institute for IT

g

You may also be interested in...

Governance of IT
Practical guidance
on how to create
a safe and robust
governance
framework.

978-1-78017-154-8

£29.99

Security Architect
Practical, effective
guidance for anyone
looking to become a
security architect.

978-1-78017-220-0

£19.99

Information Security
Management Principles
A pragmatic guide
for business
professionals and
technical experts.

978-1-78017-175-3

£24.99

www.bcs.org/bookshop

BC710/LD/AD/0414

Available in the BCS GUIDES TO IT ROLES series

Careers in IT service management:

Business Relationship Manager
Service Desk and Incident Manager
Problem Manager
Continual Service Improvement Manager

Careers in information security:

Security Architect
Information Security Auditor

Coming soon

Service Level Manager
Change Manager

http://www.bcs.org/itroles

INFORMATION
SECURITY AUDITOR

BCS, THE CHARTERED INSTITUTE FOR IT

BCS, The Chartered Institute for IT champions the global IT profession and the interests of individuals engaged in that profession for the benefit of all. We promote wider social and economic progress through the advancement of information technology, science and practice. We bring together industry, academics, practitioners and government to share knowledge, promote new thinking, inform the design of new curricula, shape public policy and inform the public.

Our vision is to be a world-class organisation for IT. Our 70,000 strong membership includes practitioners, businesses, academics and students in the UK and internationally. We deliver a range of professional development tools for practitioners and employees. A leading IT qualification body, we offer a range of widely recognised qualifications.

Further Information
BCS, The Chartered Institute for IT,
First Floor, Block D,
North Star House, North Star Avenue,
Swindon, SN2 1FA, United Kingdom.
T +44 (0) 1793 417 424
F +44 (0) 1793 417 444
www.bcs.org/contact

http://shop.bcs.org/

INFORMATION
SECURITY AUDITOR

Wendy Goucher

Published by BCS Learning & Development Ltd, a wholly owned subsidiary of BCS, The Chartered Institute for IT, First Floor, Block D, North Star House, North Star Avenue, Swindon, SN2 1FA, UK.
www.bcs.org

Paberback ISBN: 978-1-78017-216-3
PDF ISBN: 978-1-78017-217-0
ePUB ISBN: 978-1-78017-218-7
Kindle ISBN: 978-1-78017-219-4

Ebook available

British Cataloguing in Publication Data.
A CIP catalogue record for this book is available at the British Library.

Disclaimer:
The views expressed in this book are of the author(s) and do not necessarily reflect the views of the Institute or BCS Learning & Development Ltd except where explicitly stated as such. Although every care has been taken by the author(s) and BCS Learning & Development Ltd in the preparation of the publication, no warranty is given by the author(s) or BCS Learning & Development Ltd as publisher as to the accuracy or completeness of the information contained within it and neither the author(s) nor BCS Learning & Development Ltd shall be responsible or liable for any loss or damage whatsoever arising by virtue of such information or any instructions or advice contained within this publication or by any of the aforementioned.

BCS books are available at special quantity discounts to use as premiums and sale promotions, or for use in corporate training programmes. Please visit our Contact us page at www.bcs.org/contact

Typeset by Lapiz Digital Services, Chennai, India.

CONTENTS

LIST OF FIGURES

ABOUT THE AUTHOR

Wendy Goucher is an information security specialist at Goucher Consulting, an independent information security consultancy based in Scotland. She has a background in social science and a first career as a management lecturer, which lasted over 20 years before she developed her interest in the human aspect of information security into consultancy. Amongst many projects, she has helped to develop a curriculum of security awareness for children aged 5 to 18 for schools in the United Arab Emirates, and is currently involved in the development of good practice guides. She designs and delivers training and meets many other challenges where compliance and policy requirements meet operational reality.

Wendy's skill and unusual perspective on information security have enabled her to present at a number of international security conferences across the world for the Information Systems Audit and Control Association (ISACA), Gartner, the European Union Agency for Network and Information Security (ENISA) and a range of others. These events also give her the opportunity to gain insight on the implementation of security awareness in a range of cultures. This same blend of experience and insight has allowed her to become involved in a number of key projects recently, including membership of the two teams developing the BCS CESG Certified Professional Scheme and the IEEE's 'Security of the Cloud'.

As an author, Wendy maintained a regular column in *Computer Fraud and Security Magazine* for five years and still contributes on an occasional basis. She contributed to the 2012 revision of the *Information Security Management Handbook* and is currently co-authoring a book about incident management.

ABBREVIATIONS

AICPA	American Institute of Certified Public Accountants
BCCI	Bank of Credit and Commerce International
BCP	business continuity plan
BCS	BCS, The Chartered Institute for IT
BYOD	bring your own device
CBT	computer-based training
CEO	chief executive officer
CFO	chief finance officer
CIO	chief information officer
CISA	Certificate of Information Advisor
CISO	chief information security officer
CSA	Cloud Security Alliance
HIPAA	Health Insurance Portability and Accountability Act (1996; USA)
HMRC	Her Majesty's Revenue and Customs (UK)
HR	Human Resources (department)
IA	information assurance
IAASB	International Audit and Assurance Standards Board
ICO	Information Commissioner's Office (UK)

IM	incident management
IS	information security
ISACA	Information Systems Audit and Control Association
IT	information technology
ITIL	Information Technology Infrastructure Library
NIST	National Institute of Standards and Technology
OWASP	Open Web Application Security Project
PCIDSS	Payment Card Industry Data Security Standard
PEBKAC	problem exists between keyboard and chair
PSN	public services network
SFIA	Skills Framework for the Information Age (BCS)
SoX	Sarbanes Oxley Act (2002; USA)
SPF	Security Policy Framework (HM Government)
VPN	virtual private network

GLOSSARY

Compliance audit   Designed to prove to a certification authority that you meet the standards of particular scheme. This is the most common type of third party audit.

Control   A security measure that is included in a business procedure or process.

External audit   An audit that reports to an external organisation or certification body.

Governance   A set of processes and procedures by which the executive of an organisation controls the state of the organisation and gains assurance that their policies and processes are appropriate to business operations and strategy. Audit is one of the key elements of governance.

Internal audit   An audit that reports to the commissioning organisation, usually, but not always, conducted by the organisation's staff.

Penetration test   A technical test in which the defences of the organisational website, network or other digital presence are tested to identify any weaknesses.

Policy   A formal statement that sets out an organisation's method of dealing with an issue.

Procedure   A prescribed method of completing a task.

Process   A repeatable method of carrying out a business activity.

Scoping   The formal decision as to what is going to be included and excluded in an audit. Formal audits, including certification audits, often prefer to have some explanation of what is excluded.

Screenagers   Young people for whom communication, through a computer or mobile device, has been the norm from an early age. Computers and devices enable their school work as well as being a key part of the way they communicate with their friends.

Second party security audit   The key with second and third party audits is to see where the report is to be presented. If the customer organisation instigates the audit to check compliance of a supplying organisation to security requirements that have been formally agreed, and the report is made to the customer in the first instance, then this is a second party audit. For example, an organisation conducting an audit of the data centre where their network back-ups are carried out.

Security climate   A general term used to denote whether security controls, policies and procedures are generally followed within an organisation.

Security culture   The attitude and generally accepted behaviour, or norms, regarding information security within an organisation.

Third party security audit   Again, the key is to follow the report. The best way to explain a third party audit is to give an example. An organisation decides that it wants, or needs, to become compliant with an external standard such as ISO/IEC 27001:2013. The work towards compliance is internal and the costs of the audit assessment, including the costs of the external auditor, are met by the inspected company. However, the report goes to the certification body in the first instance, not the inspected organisation and it is, therefore, a third party audit.

PREFACE

'Some are born auditors, some have audit thrust upon them.'

A paraphrase of a quote from William Shakespeare's *Twelfth Night*.

There is a caricature of an information security (IS) auditor on my office wall: he is grey and sullen looking and has no shadow reflecting from the mirror next to him. I commissioned this image myself and have used it in a range of talks to IT and IS professionals and it always raises a smile. They recognise the joke; the auditor has no soul.

The image this caricature paints seems to apply to any auditor role in any profession. Auditors are the ones who require pedantic adherence to the rules, who have no understanding of the demand for innovation, thereby missing the point of business operation in the real world. Their presence can be felt to be judgemental rather than helpful as they identify issues and requirements that had not been recognised before.

However, to take these manifestations at face value is to misunderstand the role of an auditor. A key part of the role is to make sure that controls, policies and procedures actually work in the 'real world' by suggesting areas that need changes, ideally before they 'go live'.

In a way, the process of being audited can be compared to a driving examination: most people do not enjoy their driving test and the need to prove they can keep strictly to the correct driving method. I still remember that nerve-sharpening 40 minutes or so with the examiner sitting next to me in the car, watching my every move and noting every hesitation or mistake. In the lead-up to the test, and the test itself, I felt as if I was being subjected to awful and unnecessary pressure and stress. Yet, nobody would suggest we train people to drive and then rely on the police to identify those who require punishment for non-conformity. The driving examination process saves lives, and, fundamentally, all rational people agree with it.

As IS enters a phase of 'cyber' interconnectivity, information of all sorts is exposed and vulnerable to loss or deliberate attack. Such information is not confined to business documentation that has evolved from the days of the typewriter-focused office and the filing cabinet. Information might now give control of systems such as those controlling the operation of the working environment. Smart buildings can be wonderful, but they offer a new vector of attack that needs to be anticipated and defended. Audit can help to ensure that design is compliant and operationally effective.

Someone able to contribute at that edge of technological change is certainly not someone who is looking for static adherence; they have to understand what is being done and why, and its security and compliance implications.

In the course of this book I want to share my belief that good IS auditing is about balancing quality information security with operational enablement. Most of the IS auditors I know are good people, some of them are even fun people and most tell me that, while challenging, this can be a very rewarding role that makes a real contribution to the security of public and private sector business. I think that is something not said often enough.

The purpose of this book is twofold: first of all, to help those who are considering moving into an IS audit role to get a fuller feel for the personal and professional requirements as well as the career rewards it might bring. I will discuss how the role of the auditor is not only significant but also, where that individual works to achieve a high standard of professionalism, has a chance to be highly valued in modern business.

Second, it aims to help those who have audit 'thrust upon them' to get an insight into the audit process and understand how to get the best from an auditor's experience and expertise to help to make operations more secure – rather than waste time and energy banging heads with them.

To this latter group I offer these words of wisdom from *The Art of War*, Sun Tze: 'Know your enemy.'

1 INTRODUCTION TO INFORMATION SECURITY AUDITING

This book looks at information security auditing. There is much that I will talk about that could relate to any kind of auditing, because having the skill and patience to identify and review things – from the accuracy of a set of end-of-year accounts to a stock take of the books actually on the shelves in a library compared with what the record of books says should be there – takes similar skills, if very different knowledge and experience. In the case of information security auditing, what is being checked are the various elements that contribute to the defence of the information within an organisation, either by internally set business expectations or against guidelines or standards set by external bodies.

INFORMATION SECURITY

Information security (IS) is about protecting information from unauthorised access, loss or damage.

If we look at the illustration in Figure 1 we can see some of the elements that have an effect on the process of IS. From this we can see that there is a potential for tension, for example between business requirements and privacy and data protection. Ideally documents that contain sensitive personal data would have very limited access, and downloading onto a mobile device may be inhibited. But what if the sales staff need to have access to at least some customer data as they travel around seeing clients? How are those needs balanced? The answer is never easy and will arise again further through this book.

Figure 1 Elements influencing the process of information security

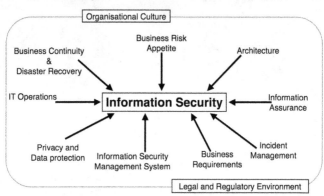

On the outside of the diagram we have Organisational Culture and Legal and Regulatory Environment. They may not feed directly into the process of IS, but they influence most, if not all, of the elements I have included here. I should say that this diagram is not definitive. There are organisations that have more or fewer elements, but these I have included show the potential range of those elements.

Since the first major data loss incident in the UK, where two discs containing sensitive personal data of thousands of customers went missing from HMRC, there has been steadily increasing pressure on organisations to be able to demonstrate the robustness of their protection of such data. Indeed, the penalties handed out by the Information Commissioner's Office (often referred to as the ICO) in the event of a data loss has expanded to include not just the large, headline-grabbing organisations, but the smaller ones too. The clear intention of such penalties is to encourage all organisations processing any kind of sensitive information to have the security of that data as a core part of their operation.

One of the elements that contribute to the resilience of the information security of an organisation is 'information assurance' (IA). This is a very important process because it gives the business owner, or board of control, knowledge regarding how the existing IS posture meets their declared business requirement. If you look at the other elements comprising IS in the diagram at Figure 1 you can see that they describe areas of activity; for example, Incident Management is about how a potential data leak is handled, while Architecture is about how the system is designed, both with operational requirements and IS in mind. Whichever of the elements you look at they are actively making a contribution to the overall protection. The odd one out is IA. This does not affect the security of information in itself, but it does look to ensure that the other elements are doing so. An auditor in the IA, or IS, area is checking the elements of the organisation against whichever criteria are seen as appropriate. Their contribution not only ensures that the elements contributing to security are present, but that they are also functional within the operational demands of normal working.

Both IS and IA roles use the same skill set, and come across many of the same problems. This book is specifically about IS, that is, checking the elements that comprise or support information protection, but in an organisation large enough to have its own audit staff they may perform both IS and IA audits. This may seem confusing, but just remember the diagram – IA is just one element of IS.

Staff may be given a short presentation on IS as part of their initial induction. However, the effectiveness of that training needs to be checked. This is important not only in terms of security, but also in terms of budget. No organisation wants to invest in training that does not lead to the required behavioural outcomes. If staff fail to understand the importance of, for example, not opening suspicious links in their email, not only could that lead to malware infection of their computer but the effort required to deal with any issues that arise from that will cost time, and time is a budget item in a modern organisation. Think how you and your colleagues would react if the network, and through it any access to the internet, shut down unexpectedly for 10 minutes in the early afternoon. Even such a short break can have a significant impact.

Another important point to note at this early stage is that quite a lot of the elements of IS are not directly IT based. Some, such as data protection, use the computer network, but are not reliant on it in the way that architecture is. Of course, a well-designed business continuity plan must be able to operate without an operational IT system, it would be one of the scenarios that is anticipated and planned for. However, ever since computers became ubiquitous in the workplace, IS has been seen as focused on IT, and often operated by the IT department. It is very important that from this point on you consider all potential aspects of IS, not just those that are based on IT activity. However, it is certainly safe to say that the overarching driver to comply with internal and external security requirements is the increasing complexity of the systems that deal with data in the modern organisation. When documents were stored in physical cabinets, access could be restricted and monitored by the cabinet owner if necessary. Documents, and therefore data, could be as safe as the organisation wished it to be, subject to its willingness to make the necessary investment in appropriate locks for cabinets and doors.

The development of computers and network access has meant that access to documents has changed drastically in the last 20 years. Therefore simply walking around the office and checking the physical security of cabinets is no longer sufficient.

In the situation of a modern organisation, the pressure for reassurance of an acceptable level of security comes from a much wider group of stakeholders than ever before. Prior to widespread office technology, the loss of sensitive information such as payroll details would be embarrassing to the company, and possibly career damaging to the responsible employee. Now the implications can be much more widespread. If data is exposed to open access the repercussions are potentially very serious – as happened in a Home Office incident in December 2013, where sensitive data relating to more than 1,500 people was published on an unrestricted spreadsheet on their website.[1] The exposed data, which included names and dates

---

[1] www.bbc.co.uk/news/uk-politics-25353311 [accessed 17 November 2015].

of birth, could potentially be used to aid a variety of cyber crimes, from 'common' fraud and theft through to terrorism at the extreme. Also, external agencies such as the ICO in the UK would need to be informed of relevant loss; that is, the loss of any data that is classified as 'sensitive' under data protection legislation. In an effort to force improvements in IS, the ICO is making increasingly clear their intention to invoke significant penalties, including publicity, on those whose careless practice leads to a significant loss of data.

These pressures mean that the assurance of security needs to be conducted thoroughly and is best overseen by someone who is not involved in the day-to-day operation of maintaining data security. This 'outsider' can have a more systematic view of operations and can work with staff to highlight risk and give guidance as to appropriate and acceptable methods to handle that risk.

Now, let us pause again to emphasise some important points. I have mentioned 'both internal and external security requirements'. The point of origin for security audits can be internal, maybe as part of a scheduled review programme, or external, in order to demonstrate compliance with some external standards. It is carried out by an employee of the organisation. Some audits are external, which means that they are carried out by someone who is not a member of staff. In most cases the audit is likely to test for conformity to an external standard, such as ISO 27000. In some cases, however, it may be to test for conformity to guidelines set by another organisation, such as a client. For example, if an organisation is using the services of a cloud service provider, they may wish the provider to supply evidence of their conformity to standards that are internal to the customer's organisation. Whatever the circumstances, the auditor checking the adherence needs the same skills and faces similar challenges.

So, before we go further, let us just check that we have two possible points of confusion clear:

- An IS auditor reviews the various elements that comprise the way the organisation deals with the protection of its data. An IA auditor looks at how the current operation of security in the organisation meets the business risk appetite of the organisation.

- An internal audit is when the auditor is an employee of the organisation they are reviewing. An external audit is when the auditor is not an employee of the organisation they are reviewing.

Key tenets

Ever since communication progressed from being purely speech to being expressed in a physical form such as writing or recording the spoken word, people have worked to protect some information by following, whether they realised it or not, three key tenets; these are confidentiality, integrity and availability.

Confidentiality

Confidentiality is what we normally mean by something being kept 'secret' in that it restricts who has access to information. When I was a child, a popular way of ensuring confidentiality of your private thoughts was to write them in a notebook or diary that could be locked with a key. You then kept that key in a very safe place. The same process is achieved on a computer by placing a password on the access to a document or folder. Of course, this password should be one that is not shared or easily guessed, much like my diary lock had to be a good strong one and the key hidden where it was too hard for the curious to find.

Confidentiality can be important for a range of reasons. The information may be sensitive, the sort of information that could cause embarrassment, or it might be exploited against the person it concerns in some way. In everyday life we trust doctors, priests and even all those faceless people at our banks with details of our lives that we do not want widely known.

One of the problems with social media is that users often place too much trust on its ability to keep information confidential. There are many anecdotes giving examples of people including acquaintances such as work colleagues and even line managers, rather than just good or close friends, in friendship groups on Facebook. This means that expressions of frustration with regard to work can be read more widely than was intended.

VIRGIN FLIGHT CREW INSULT PASSENGERS

In October 2008, in a case that quickly became infamous, 13 members of Virgin's staff were sacked for getting involved in a discussion group on Facebook that became a forum for expressing their opinions of some passengers, the cleanliness of their aircraft and even the airworthiness of some planes.[2] Clearly, members of the group believed that they were expressing their frustrations in a protected environment that would restrict access and, in essence, remain private. The fact that the discussion was revealed both to the media and to Virgin itself demonstrates that they were wrong. Interestingly, in the report referenced here, Virgin say that there are appropriate channels for concerns to be aired. In other words, their dismissals were not particularly about them holding damaging opinions, but that they did not keep them confidential. In failing in that way they brought Virgin, and all its staff, into disrepute. Confidentiality, or the breaking of it, can have huge impacts on concerned parties.

Integrity

Integrity is about information being unaltered, except by an authorised person. To take an extreme example, if an international peace treaty was accidentally openly shared

---

[2] www.telegraph.co.uk/travel/3332031/Virgin-sacks-cabin-crew-for-insulting-passengers-on-Facebook.html [accessed 23 February 2015].

online so that people could freely change elements without the changes being obvious, then the final document would lack credibility in that form. Neither side could trust that the terms to which they agreed were those originally negotiated without careful checking. Recently there was a situation where hackers broke into the computer systems at Chopin Airport, near Warsaw in Poland. These systems were responsible for issuing flight plans to aircraft of the Polish airliner, LOT, and all of the planes affected were grounded until the integrity of the information issued by the systems could be assured once again.[3]

This does make it sound very serious, and indeed it is, especially in an engineering context. When it comes to information, 'integrity' is more closely aligned with trust. To get a definition of this word I first went to the *Oxford English Dictionary* (OED) because I could trust that the definitions it contains are a correct explanation of its use in British English. If someone were to hack the OED and change some of the spellings to American English, then the integrity of the information contained in the dictionary would be undermined until it could be thoroughly checked to remove the rogue spellings. Until that could be done, the trust users have in the information the dictionary provides would be significantly harmed.

In any situation where it is essential that users trust the integrity of information they are able to access, integrity is a high priority for those maintaining and overseeing systems.

If we think back to the widespread use of cheques as a payment method, the cheque owner had to write the amount to be transferred on the presentation of the cheque in both words and numbers. This was a simple way to prevent the easiest of frauds, that of the receiver carefully changing the figures on the form in order to

---

[3] www.wired.com/2015/06/airlines-security-hole-grounded-polish-planes/ [accessed 14 September 2015].

cash it for a higher amount than intended. It could be argued that 'integrity' is the silent risk, because it is often forgotten. When we struggled to fill in a cheque with a thin pen and cold fingers, and a growing queue of customers behind, the need to write out the amount in full mostly seemed a silly waste of time. In fact it was protecting the integrity of the transaction.

Availability

Availability means that users can trust that they can access important information quickly.

This is important in many different situations. Within most organisations the cost of an unplanned disruption in the availability of the IT network can quickly build. There is the cost of people being paid to do work that they are unable to do. The cost of key information not being available to complete a project on time may cause penalty clauses to be activated. There may be overtime costs for staff working anti-social hours to find and rectify the problem as quickly as possible. If the organisation is a particularly critical one, such as in a healthcare provision situation, there may even be a threat to life if patient records are inaccessible.

In a retail business the cost of a website – or even the payment facility on a website – being unavailable can be huge. Well-known retailers may lose a potential sale to a rival, as customers do not want to wait for the site to come back; however, they may have built up enough brand loyalty that there is a good chance the customer will eventually return. There would also need to be a significant number of lost customers to have a big financial impact. However, where the profit margin is small then the loss of even a few customers, even assuming they return in the medium term, is likely to be much bigger.

INFORMATION SECURITY IN THE WORLD OF WORK

More information is moved faster and further than ever before, and a good deal of that will be sensitive in some way, whether it is personal or corporate. That being the case, the principle of assuring the safety of the information throughout the entire process is not only essential but also needs to be responsive to changing tools and business and operational needs.

In this modern world, IS has a new challenge. It pulls against the received wisdom of the last 30 years, namely that IS is essentially a technical IT problem with an IT solution. In fact, the way policy and procedures are both designed and implemented are essential elements of security, and these are mostly dependent on the awareness, evaluation and actions of users. The importance of the human element has been known for a long time. In 2006 it was possible for Intel to use the acronym PEBKAC (problem exists between keyboard and chair) in their online advertising, firm in the knowledge that their target audience would understand. Indeed it can be said that some IS professionals believe in the sense behind the equation:

information security = IT security + blaming the user

The IS professional, especially one with audit responsibility, needs to look at IS controls in the context of business requirements as this will give the best insight into any operational weakness.

The need to assure the operational effectiveness of IS is not new, and neither is the need to check the procedures that ensure that security. The role of the person who is tasked to audit the IS controls, policies and procedures will be discussed in greater detail when we look at a model auditor in Chapter 2. Next we will look at auditing itself.

WHAT IS INFORMATION SECURITY AUDITING?

The information security auditor, whether internal or external to the organisation, has the key task of monitoring and evaluating the various elements of IS. This can be a very challenging task as some elements will actively impact on others, and understanding how that works is vital to giving the most effective view on the operation of security.

In order to carry out an audit it is helpful if the IS auditor is aware of the context, both internal and external, in which the various elements are devised and operated. This can be a challenge, not least because there is likely to be a variety of approaches for the different elements comprising the IS defence. For example, the reasons for, and funding of, incident management may be very different from standard IT operations. While most organisations have some form of IT operations, setting up and maintaining an incident management (IM) capability is a conscious decision. Often this is a reaction to realising the impact of an incident in another, comparable organisation. This is not a bad reason for starting with IM, but, as time goes on, if there are no significant incidents the rationale may lose power and investment.

It is important with additional elements, such as IM, that the auditor who is evaluating its capability is aware of both the reason for its instigation and any change in the associated business risk appetite. IM teams can be quite expensive to set up, train and maintain to an effective standard. If the perceived risk has fallen low enough that senior management are content to accept the risk of not continuing to have this provided internally, they are likely to stop doing so. They may decide to use an external provider, or simply move the responsibility for provision to the IT department. The auditor will be most effective if they can understand the reason for that decision. They can then bring their knowledge and experience to supporting that change or highlighting issues that do not appear to have been addressed.

TYPES OF AUDIT

There are two basic types of audit: an internal audit and an external audit. While the process is similar, if not nearly identical, the objectives of the exercise and the scope may be very different.

Internal audit

This is driven internally and generally instigated at the behest of management or board level requirements. An internal review can be as narrow as a single operational area, such as a new system or facility, or as broad as the entire organisation. It is worth saying at this point that the holistic nature of modern organisations, with departments, divisions and other groupings being much less isolated than in the past, means that most areas of any organisation connect in some way with many others. It can often be helpful, therefore, for more than one area to have their operation audited in the same project as any changes required in one area may impact on, or be impacted by, those in others.

The fact that this is an internal audit does not mean that it is necessarily less rigorous than an external one. Indeed, someone carrying out an internal audit is more likely to have some knowledge of a business' weaknesses (or 'where the bodies are buried') so they can focus on areas of weakness and concern, which can lead to a greater amount of work required to deal with those issues.

The frameworks used for an internal audit often reflect existing or proposed external audit requirements. For example, if the organisation is expecting to seek accreditation under the ISO/IEC 27002 or is considering using the COBIT 5 framework in the medium term, it is reasonable to use that framework documentation as a guideline to their development beforehand. More details of these and other frameworks, both why and how they are used, can be found in Chapter 3. Suffice to say at this point that using a pre-existing framework can mean that the work eventually required to achieve accreditation can be reduced as the documentation, and possibly some of the processes, are already in place and producing evidence of operation.

It is the nature of an external audit that the aim in reviewing the system in advance is to ensure that it complies with the external requirements. However, with an internal audit, a key question is: Is the system fit for purpose? This 'purpose' will be defined at senior level and will include operational needs, which mean that the organisation functions efficiently, as well as security requirements. This means that not only must the security controls and processes be good, they must also work in the everyday activity of business operations. If a control takes more skill or effort than the user is willing or able to contribute, then it will be circumvented and the effort of devising it is wasted. It is as pointless as the oft-used picture of the security gates on a dirt track with no fence or walls either side. There may have been a good reason for having the gate, but the tyre tracks in the mud showed that drivers were simply working around it.

Trying to meet the requirements of both security and operations can be very problematic. Indeed it is arguably amongst the biggest challenges to any IS team. One of the roles the auditor can play is to use their experience and knowledge of both operations and the frameworks being used to advise those with that task. However, it should be stressed that an internal audit is carried out at the instigation of the organisation itself so that it can identify areas of concern, and set in place programmes to tackle them, without having to conform to the requirements if senior managers are willing to accept the shortfall.

To slightly complicate this issue there is a sub-set of internal audit, and that is a second party audit, which is one demanded by a customer to satisfy their internal security requirements. This differs from an external audit in that it does not need to be against any external framework or standard. Who conducts the audit in this case can vary, and is often dictated by the reason why the audit is being carried out. If it is because the customer has external compliance requirements, such as from the Financial Services Authority, it is more likely that they will feel that they want to conduct the audit themselves, or nominate someone to do so on their behalf. If the customer wants an audit to reassure their stakeholders, then they may be able to accept an audit conducted entirely internally against guidelines they have provided. This will need to be attested to at a sufficiently senior level in the audited organisation. Where a second party audit is going to be required on a regular basis, there is a need for a good relationship with that customer to ensure a clear understanding of their requirements. This means that the contracting company should be made aware if any changes to policy or controls might cause an impact on the client relationship and this therefore needs to be discussed with them in advance. If the framework itself is specific, then the person auditing the operation will need to spend more time ensuring that they have entirely understood how it fits in the organisational context; otherwise it is more likely that impacts might be missed. Therefore, any adjustments that are identified at the time of routine audit are likely to cause additional expense as extra care, and checking, will be required. This could make such audits potentially more time consuming for the contractor. The supplying contractors' organisations would be well advised to read their contracts with great care[4] to make sure they factor such costs into their budget for the work.

In the wake of the high-profile data leak incidents in 2008, one financial institution in the UK decided to ensure that their ability to make auditing site visits to suppliers who provided key services linked to data security (such as those providing secure disposal for paper and hardware) was included in the contract. The clause was explicitly highlighted to the supplier in order to avoid any possible doubt and site visits were scheduled either six-monthly or annually, depending on the sensitivity of the data or how varied or changeable that process could be. The requirement for these audit visits put a great burden on the inspecting team, as well as those being inspected. It was therefore important that a good relationship was developed between the parties to avoid 'surprises' (with changes to the supplying contractor's processes discussed, and agreed, at the planning stage) and to allow for the inspections to go smoothly. The financial institution is sufficiently large, and its requirement for external contractors sufficiently wide, that the process for carrying out these inspections can be huge.

---

[4] Of course, it should go without saying that one should always read any contract with care.

Every audit inspection, even routine ones, needs planning, the inspection itself carried out and a report written and discussed with all parties. If anomalies arise then they need to be discussed and an agreement reached as to how the issues are best addressed. In the light of all this work it is clear that those suppliers who present no problems at audit are going to have a better relationship with the customer and a better chance of the contract being renewed. Obviously, suppliers who do not make themselves aware of the customer's requirements, so that they can be considered in any changes, will have a more problematic relationship with their customer and be more likely to be replaced should another supplier approach the customer.

In addition – and this is a particular problem with internal audit – it can be difficult to notice weaknesses because staff have developed their working approach around them. In some cases, working around a strong control can make working lives sufficiently easier such that a security weakness posed by the 'work-around' might be overlooked. For example, the introduction of the ban on smoking in public buildings, which was introduced in Scotland in 2006 and in 2007 in England and Wales, meant that staff need to leave the building to smoke. Where this happens in a building with strong access controls, such as a single point of entry requiring a card swipe or other authenticating action, or just having to walk a long way to get to the main entrance, an alternative solution is often found. In many cases, smokers go out of a fire door. To make sure that they do not then have to make the extra journey to the main entrance to re-enter, especially in warm weather, the door is propped open with a fire extinguisher. This makes an easy entrance point for any skilled social engineer. An internal auditor needs to ensure that they are alert to these everyday security vulnerabilities.

External audit

External audit is required where an organisation needs to achieve accreditation against a recognised standard such as the Payment Card Industry Data Security Standard (PCIDSS) or ISO/IEC 22301. This might be carried out because of current customer requirements, or in the expectation that said accreditation will allow new customers, with more stringent requirements, to be courted. This differs from a second party audit in that an external audit needs to be accredited to a recognised certification and audited by an impartial, external auditor. While a second party may require that the contracting supplier has particular aspects of their processes audited to align with, for example ISO/IEC 27001, the supplier would be audited internally, or by the customer.

Such compliance projects, especially with established organisations, are best started internally with a team involving an internal auditor or someone with experience of being audited under that accreditation. The external auditor can be contacted at any point of the preparation phase, for example, in order to check the acceptability of a proposed control. Unlike internal auditors, external auditors tend to work with several organisations at the same time, which means that they do not have the personal knowledge of the working of the organisation that an internal auditor has, but could have a broader experience. It is important to establish a good relationship with the external auditor, as with the customer conducting second party audits, for very much the same reasons. Nobody wants surprises when it comes to the actual audit as these can lead to remediating actions that are problematic to normal operations.

As has been said, external audits are often embarked on initially because of stakeholder or customer pressure to be assured about the security of the systems and processes of the organisation. This means that the pressure is really on as business, or potential business, can be at stake. If the organisation fails to achieve the required compliance, it is likely to have a significant impact on the operations until that can be rectified. In an ideal situation, an internal audit would be carried out first in order to identify where compliance gaps are. This can help with planning and budgeting for the full compliance audit. However, where this is not possible, an external compliance programme could sometimes have to be run on a very tight budget. In this situation the external auditor needs to be clear and consistent in their guidance.

Miscommunication can lead to frustration and potentially wasted time and effort. It also makes the work of the internal team driving the compliance project very much harder.

AUDITING STAGES

In most cases the purpose of an IS audit review is to evaluate the operational security of the overall organisation. For an audit to be fully effective it is important to have a systematic approach ensuring that all relevant processes are included. It is best to think of the process of IS auditing as a series of stages, some taking longer than others, but each building on the work already done. There are a number of different approaches to staging the IS audit process, some more specific to particular types of organisation, and some containing a lot of detail; however, most reflect that well-known process: Plan, Do, Check, Act. So let us look at each of these in turn and fill in some of the detail that may be relevant to your business.

Plan

External frameworks such as ISO/IEC 27001[5] and COBIT 5[6] prepare their scope in a way that will give assurance to all stakeholders, which can be challenging. It is possible to achieve accreditation under ISO/IEC 27001 and still not satisfy a potential client because the scope does not include an area that is of particular concern to them. Therefore this planning stage needs to be approached with care and to utilise the experience of both audit and non-audit staff. The scope can cause some surprises to organisations or staff approaching it for the first time. For example, it is most likely to require input from areas that might not expect to be included, say, facilities management as they have information and control regarding the physical protection of the buildings involved. Concerns can range from physical access controls, to the quality of the locks and other perimeter controls, to incident logging and monitoring

_____

[5] www.iso.org/iso/home/standards/management-standards/iso27001.htm [accessed 17 March 2015].

[6] www.isaca.org/cobit/pages/default.aspx [accessed 17 March 2015].

of access for out-of-hours contractors such as maintenance and cleaning. With organisations of all sizes taking advantage of off-site storage in data centres, many will decide that they need to include some level of assessment of the security of these premises. Thankfully, increasing demand for this sort of evidence means that data centres are finding that they need to be able to demonstrate compliance to TIA 942, which helps to promote their business. This can mean that, for non-critical data handling, customers presented with an appropriately scoped accreditation document may be spared the need to inspect the premises themselves. The IS auditor will be a valuable asset to this project, especially if they are included from this first stage.

This is especially important if an audit is being carried out with a tight deadline, for example at the request of a significant customer. It can be tempting to shortcut the planning stage, perhaps to follow a process used before. However, technology and business process can change frequently so it is important to clearly outline the scope of the audit each time it is carried out – i.e. clearly set out what is to be included and what left out. It is useful to have a record of the rationale behind any areas of exclusion just in case those reading the final report query this.

The scope for an audit may focus on a particular area of operation; for example, ensuring secure practice with regard to handling particularly sensitive information such as research and development data. It may appear initially that the way the data is processed by the user is the key area. However, the scope will also need to include the use, movement, retention, back-up and storage of that data.

Those devising the scope need to be mindful of current threats to similar organisations to themselves. There are a number of annual threat reviews that are released by vendors and looking through a few of these, especially from vendors who provide different services or hardware, can ensure that trends can be identified; for example, the Price Waterhouse Coopers (PWC) annual security breach report.[7]

---

[7] www.pwc.co.uk/audit-assurance/publications/2014-information-security-breaches-survey.jhtml [accessed 27 March 2015].

A good scope will also look forward towards developments in operational practice that might reasonably be expected. For example, when the iPad was first introduced, few organisations anticipated the impact that the combination of the user-friendly nature of the device and the economic slump making budgets very restricted would have. The user-friendly nature of the tablet device meant that many bought their own to use at work as well as home thus giving rise to the 'bring your own device' (BYOD) phenomenon. The subsequent security issues were 'hot topics' in IS presentation and discussion for a good while after the tablet appeared. However, for most it was a case of closing the gate after the horse had bolted, because BYOD was established and security was playing 'catch-up'. No security operation wants to be in that position.

While looking outwards to threats, good planning also looks inwards and takes into account any particular data types or processes that are regarded as critical. A critical process might include the processing of wages and salaries. The tolerance of a process failure that delays payments to staff is likely to be very low. Many people have key payments set to automatically move from their bank account as soon as possible after they are paid. If there is a delay, that could mean that, for example, a mortgage payment is missed, which could have both financial and psychological pressures. An example of this happened in January 2015 to staff at the retail chain River Island[8] as the result of a 'computer glitch'. Of course, with modern social media staff do not only get to grumble and complain to their colleagues and family, they can also complain to the world. This then hits at the reputation of the company and is unlikely to be well received by stakeholders.

Once the scoping has been devised, and checked against any accreditation requirements that the organisation must be mindful of, the planning of the audit project can commence. As with any project, this will need to be given a timescale and have a manager in charge who has the authority required to access the information they need. It is also essential that the

---

[8] www.thenorthernecho.co.uk/news/11700097.River_Island_staff_face_pay_delay/?ref=mr [accessed 28 March 2015].

overall audit review be sanctioned at board level. This will help to prevent log-jams that can come from delays such as additional, unexpected budget requirements.

A programme will also need to be created that allows for meetings and interviews of those holding key roles for the audit; for example, the IT network manager. Physical access may be required to some areas including some within the standard office environment, external storage venues, server rooms and others. In most cases the relevant people need to be available to answer any queries and discuss any issues that may arise. The availability of these people may significantly impact the programme, and this is one of the points where having positive backing from board level can make a difference. It can raise significantly the priority of co-operating with the audit.

In summary, the Plan stage includes:

1. Defining the scope of the audit.
2. Identifying relevant threats.
3. Identifying key assets that must be secured.
4. Defining any business requirements of the audit.
5. Outlining a timetable for the audit process.
6. Identifying key people, or roles, that the auditor will need to speak to in carrying out the audit.
7. Identifying any personnel who are external to the business, but would have information vital to the audit. These include external contractors.
8. Ensuring that external parties are aware of the audit and the role they are expected to play in it.
9. Agreeing the format of the audit report and any particular circumstances surrounding the presentation of the report; for example, that it must be presented to the executive board at the last meeting before the end of the financial year, or at the AGM.

Do

After all the planning, carrying out the actual audit can seem to be the most straightforward part of the process. It is certainly at this point that good planning will pay its dividend. However, it is important to appreciate that in most situations you, as the auditor, are going to be more interested in gathering information than the person you are talking to is. It is helpful to consider that you performing an audit, even a routine one, can be interpreted as threatening, especially if there is uncertainty in the organisation, for example regarding potential restructuring, as in this sort of uncertain situation you collecting information could be construed as part of a process of identifying people for possible redundancy. In this sort of situation it is important that senior management are prepared to give a written assurance of the purpose of the audit to any staff members who are concerned about the effect of their co-operation.

The scope of the audit will, by its nature, define how it is carried out. It may take a largely passive form whereby the presence of key components is recorded, for example, establishing the existence of an Access Control Policy. It may be necessary either to carry out more pro-active testing, such as an exercise in restoration of the system from back-up, or use results from a recent test carried out on the system.

It may be necessary to:

- Identify and manage network access controls.
- Evaluate intrusion detection processes.
- Identify identity and access management process.
- Investigate the back-up process, including the program for checking the rebooting of the network from back-up.
- Investigate the process for filtering and monitoring email activity.
- Investigate all relevant sites in terms of the physical vulnerability.

In summary, the Do stage includes:

1. Holding a meeting of relevant parties to identify any changes that have emerged since the planning stage.
2. Making any adjustments to the original plan that are now required.
3. Checking that the plan is still a valid representation of the audit required.
4. Firming up the timetable including meetings and delivery points.
5. Identifying any external issues that might affect the deliverability according to timetable.
6. Carrying out the audit.

Check

This is the stage where the information collected is brought together to be fed back to the organisation. This initially takes the form of a draft report that is issued for discussion. It is essential that this stage takes place because there can be a number of legitimate reasons why information given to the auditor might be inaccurate or misleading; for example, if the person providing the information is new to their role or has just come back from an extended period on secondment to another division of the company. In this sort of case the person giving the information may be giving the information in good faith, while being unaware of recent changes. Circulating the draft at this stage can also give those concerned the opportunity to make minor changes that will deal with an issue raised.

While the draft stage is important, it is also important that it not be allowed to drag on too long as it can become out of date.

In summary the Check stage includes:

1. Presenting the draft report.
2. Discussing the findings with relevant parties.
3. Fixing minor issues if necessary.

4. Beginning work to address any critical issues that impact on priority assets if necessary.

5. Providing clarification to the organisation.

Act

This stage starts with the delivering of the final report. This can include the presentation of key findings to the board in order that they have the opportunity to discuss the findings with the auditor.

There then needs to be agreement on the prioritisation of dealing with the issues that arise. It is possible that this may have started as soon as the issue was reported in the draft, and therefore at this point progress can be reported.

Where issues arise that are considered by senior management to be of lower priority then discussion of the rationale behind that decision can be recorded in the minutes of any meeting so any subsequent review of the audit action points can understand the reasoning behind that decision.

It is important that this is not seen as the final part of the audit. Audit is most effective when it is dynamic, in that actions are discussed and carried out and at a later date those actions reviewed in the light of the audit report. If the information from an audit is allowed to become 'shelf-ware' then time, effort of both of the auditor and of internal staff assisting them and the cost of carrying out the work, is all wasted. It is important, therefore, that a review of the agreed critical changes be scheduled. This may involve the auditor or be reviewed by internal staff. The result of the review should also be recorded so that it is available at the next audit.

In summary, the Act stage includes:

1. Delivering the final report.

2. Discussing the findings of the report.

3. Prioritising issues to be addressed.

4. Agreeing and timetabling actions.

5. Agreeing to a future review of critical changes.

THE BUSINESS BENEFITS OF IS AUDITS

'Remember that an audit is not something that is done to you, but with you.'[9]

There is no denying the fact that having your work, and the work of your team, scrutinised by a third party to check if it is in keeping with the rules can be stressful and frustrating. Everyone in an organisation has their job to do; in many cases employees may believe that they have a workload more appropriate for 1½ people rather than just one. Then along comes a directive from 'on high' that the system must be prepared for audit. Not just one more task, but potentially a huge one. This could mean that an 'internal audit assessor' role joining your responsibilities could be as welcome as flu at Christmas. But maybe we just need to better appreciate what IS auditing is about, and especially how early insight can make change more efficient and effective and the business benefits it brings.

Customers and potential customers

If the business benefits of the audit are not clear to those participating, it can easily be perceived as a waste of time and, worse still, the bringer of stress to staff, thereby lowering morale and reducing efficiency of general working. The risk of this negativity is greater with an internal audit as there is often no obvious external reason to justify or even blame for the disruption. It is important, therefore, that the benefits to the business of the audit process are appreciated by all who have to participate.

Perhaps the clearest benefit is when the audit process is leading to external accreditation. This can help to retain existing customers, whose stakeholders may require increased, verifiable care to be taken with their data. It may also open the door to potential customers who have the requirement for external accreditation for all suppliers. This is, perhaps, the easiest justification for the disruption of audit. Most staff will be attuned to the need to retain and acquire customers.

---

[9] Basu, 2008.

In this modern, computerised age there can be few organisations that do not use and store digital data. Where this data is clearly sensitive or private, such as HR records, one would hope that the data is being protected appropriately, probably with co-operation between HR and IT departments. However, especially in smaller organisations, security can be functional. I mean by this that it is a process or an action designed to protect or, for example, enable secure access to sensitive data.

Security culture

One of the benefits of IS audits is to help bring information security into focus for the whole business, rather than in semi-autonomous fiefdoms. The most effective protection of any organisation comes when protection encompasses all aspects of its operation. That also means that it includes the way staff do their work as well as technical controls. Secure practice can be the hardest aspect of security to implement. Practices have to be user-friendly enough that users see the point of making the effort to use them. They also work best if everyone is following the same practices. This means that staff are encouraged by their colleagues to carry out their activities in a secure manner. This integration of secure practice into day-to-day operations in an acceptable way, is generally what people mean when they say their organisation has a 'security culture'. Making secure practice in work part of 'the way we do things here' has often been found to be more effective than any other method of persuasion, including financial incentives. If all staff understand the risk that insecurity brings and believe that things that they do can make a real difference to the 'battle', then they are more likely to encourage each other in taking up and making secure practice into a routine or habitual way of working. There is a lot of good recent research around that seeks to understand how to optimise IS training and education, often based on experiments and projects carried out in real organisations. Goo, Yim and Kim[10] in their survey of members of the

---

[10] Goo et al., 2013.

Information Technology Service Management Forum,[11] stated that: 'The information security climate has significant positive influence on the intention of security policy compliance.'

By 'security climate' they mean the background to the security culture of an organisation. Where the organisation has IS as a high priority, the security culture will seek to encourage the development of a sound security policy. This will influence the way security awareness training is carried out as well as the attitude of the senior board to investment of the sort that might encourage a positive attitude to security. Many larger organisations, for example, offer discounted, or free, antivirus software for staff to use on their personal computers and devices. This helps to protect the organisation in the event that the employee uses that equipment for business, but it also encourages staff to appreciate that security is important in all aspects of communication. I would add a note of caution to the discussion of 'security culture'. That is that this works best where secure practice is integrated into the normal processes of business operation. Where it is an additional process it is more likely to be overlooked or forgotten. Security culture therefore needs to be implicit in the overall culture of the organisation to be most effective.

Lubricating the security budget

Some IS professionals I have spoken to suggest that having an IS audit carried out on an organisation brings focus, including that of those with budgetary control, to secure practice. When that happens and dialogues about secure practice and operational issues start, then that can lead to the need for additional investment, such as encrypted USB sticks. Ordinarily it can be difficult to demonstrate value for money in investment in IS; for example, how do you demonstrate that giving all executives privacy screens for their tablet devices increases protection against 'shoulder surfing' or screen capture by

---

[11] The itSMF is an independent, not for profit organisation founded in 1991 that actively involves itself in the development and promotion of best practice, standards and qualifications in the IT Service Management arena.

camera? Such 'loss' might not ever be recognised, so how can an improvement be recognised? Where an IS audit is being conducted, such an investment can fulfil the function of demonstrating an overall commitment to secure operations by the business, and thereby provide some budgetary justification.

Management 'buy-in' to security

Linked to this is the fact that an IS audit should require involvement of all levels of management. In the aftermath of the financial collapse of Lehman Brothers in 2008 it is no longer acceptable for senior management to deny knowledge or responsibility for corporate governance,[12] and that includes responsibility for the safety of data. The first version of ISO 27001:2005 had a strong element that was seeking to ensure senior and board level managers' involvement in securing the business process. The new version, ISO 27001:2013, moves on and pushes for engagement from the middle level of management who have, apart from the higher risk departments such as IT or HR, been able to pay less attention to security thus far. It is clear that those who worked at the revision of the standard were looking to use it as a tool for promoting a culture of security throughout organisations; this means those who prepare, and implement any kind of audit, have an important role to play. Where an audit is performed, whether internal or external, it is important that senior staff are not only cited as responsible in the documentation presented, but are also able to demonstrate their awareness of that responsibility to the auditor.

As has already been said, if at least the managerial level of the organisation has a positive appreciation of the ultimate benefit of audit, then less time and energy tend to be wasted fighting it.

There are two basic approaches that people take to prepare for audit, especially external audit resulting in accreditation, and the difference lies in the emphasis.

---

[12] http://thoughtmanagement.org/2012/06/26/rbs-vs-lehman-brothers-failures-in-leadership-culture-and-regulators/ [accessed 18 November 2015].

Short-term gain

The aim of the audit could simply be to pass, ideally with minimum cost of time and money. We often find companies who have found themselves in a position where they have to become accredited quickly due to pressure from external stakeholders. It may be that they do not have the luxury or planned budget or spare personnel hours to complete the task in the way they would like at that point. Sometimes they express the intention to invest more in preparing for re-accreditation. Some even do so. We find that this situation brings the greatest stress and the least satisfaction to all involved. It takes a major effort of will to push forward after accreditation to continue improvements and the planning of future improvements. It often reminds me of the student who always leaves their essay until the day or the night before the hand-in time. I have seen many students find themselves frantically fighting to get work in with so little time left to deal with unexpected problems. Many have handed work in to me, looked me in the eye and said that they will never, ever do that again: 'Next time I will hand in the week before, no way will I go through that again.' The vast majority of them are back next term with a familiarly stressed look and a dash for the deadline. Some seem to need the adrenalin rush of an approaching deadline, most just underestimate how many things they are trying to do at the same time. They simply do not have the time to take their time. That latter situation is the one I have seen reflected with clients. They want to take time, but they just do not have the time to do so.

It is best to think of the short-term approach as picking up a 'fad diet' such as the Cabbage Diet. Close adherence to the rules for the diet can bring significant results in terms of weight loss. The problem is they do not generally address why the dieter is larger than they would like to be. If their problem is lifestyle (or their personal culture if you like) then the weight is not going to stay off unless they make a fundamental change to the way they live their lives.

A friend of mine wanted to lose weight for her son's wedding so she looked good in the photographs, which is a very laudable ambition. She achieved her goal by eating a low carbohydrate diet, going swimming every morning (which took over an hour out of her day) plus various exercise classes three or four times a week. She achieved her goal, lost two dress sizes and looked great. However, once the target was past, although her eating remained quite healthy, the regular trips to the gym reduced through the winter and minor injury setbacks, and the exercise classes stopped all together. Within a year she had returned to her original size. It was a short-term fix that achieved a short-term target; and one that was very important to her. What it was not was the beginning of her life as a slimmer person because the actions she had taken were unsustainable in the medium to long term. Too often, passing an audit is a very similar exercise to dieting. Huge effort is put into establishing policies and procedures that will satisfy the requirements of passing the audit.

Longer-term investment

On the other hand there are those organisations who are in a position to use the audit as part of the development of the operational processes as a whole. In this case the audit and the process of accreditation can provide a check of the overall design and implementation of procedures and policies. This in turn can help to make them more operationally secure and therefore acceptable at audit and onwards. This situation is most likely to arise when the project leader has the experience and knowledge to see the benefit of early preparation, including the checking of procedures and system designs against proposed accreditation criteria. They also need the authority to make the investment in accreditable equipment and processes. Where the organisation is in a position to take a longer-term approach, this is more likely to help sustain stability in systems as the requirement to change fundamental elements of the systems or processes is less likely. Also, some processes that are labour-intensive to maintain, such as user privilege management, are more likely to be incorporated into normal practice where a longer-term approach to accreditation is taken. This can otherwise be given a lower priority attention as the threat being protected against, provided good exit procedures are in place, is an internal one. Few organisations like to acknowledge focus on the internal threat to data security as that might be regarded as distrusting staff. However, if such processes are all part of an overall strategy, this impression can be reduced as secure practice becomes part of 'the way we do things here': i.e. security culture.

Another aspect of a longer-term approach is less wasted effort, or at least more effective use of effort. I asked my colleague for an example of policies that fall into disuse as soon as the auditor leaves the room and he said that the dustiest shelf-wares in most organisations are the business continuity plan (BCP) and the incident management (IM) procedures. If the organisation does not have a core and regular requirement for these documents,[13] they probably do not see the light of day between audit and the time to prepare for the audit review. They are very unlikely to be rehearsed on a regular basis, as would be good practice. These have not become part of operational routine or habit, so it is most likely their practice will wither and die. This is, if not acceptable, then reasonable, if the point of the audit is just to achieve accreditation. If the organisation wants real protection from rare, but potentially catastrophic, events then they need to keep these processes dusted.

HOT TIP FOR AUDITORS

If you read a BCP or a IM plan and it seems to have a generic tone, it is likely that this has either been written by a single person or small team with minimal input, and therefore without 'buy-in' from the organisation as a whole. It will need not only its own dust jacket, but a little blanket to keep out the cold. It is not going to know the comfort of human contact.

---

[13] If these documents were physical then those in the major financial organisations in the UK, especially high profile ones like banks, would be rather dog-eared.

The positive leader effect

Although circumstances surrounding an audit can influence how the process is received by staff, a bigger element is the attitude and action of the project leader. A positive leader in an audit project will use the resources they have, including the skills and knowledge of the staff around them. They will guide and encourage the team through the tough work that goes into audit. They will have good dialogue with internal and external auditors in order that the planning process is a sound foundation. They need to be brave in facing unwelcome issues, clear headed and determined. They also need to have a longer vision to ensure that staff are rewarded for their effort by processes that better fit with the operational requirements of the business. Also, by encouraging the maintenance of the peripheral elements examined in the audit, they provide the assurance and protection that is intended.

Not forgetting the IS auditor

Although the positive contributions of IS audit is mentioned in a number of places in this book, it is also important, I think, to make sure they are mentioned here. A key element in ensuring an IS audit makes a positive contribution to business practice is the professionalism of the auditor. At their best they will challenge the way that the organisation works in order that it not only presents the appearance of security, but also has secure practice at the core of its day-to-day operations. Taking on that challenge is when IS auditors, both internal and external, really can begin to make a real contribution towards making an organisation work optimally.

2 THE ROLE OF THE INFORMATION SECURITY AUDITOR

It is the role of the IS auditor to check the policies and processes of information security in normal business operations.

The IS auditor is there to provide an overview and facilitate secure operations, and this applies equally if they are an internal or external auditor. Their help may come in discussions with various parts of the organisation, or it may be in presenting issues that are significant to secure operations and that may have had insufficient attention from the levels of the hierarchy that may be able to help find solutions.

To this end, an IS auditor needs up-to-date knowledge and understanding of the business process, as well an awareness of potential issues that are emerging that may need to be considered by the organisation.

THE GULF OF EXECUTION

Research suggests that there is a gap between the behaviour that users genuinely intend to follow and what they do in practice. This is sometimes known as the 'Gulf of Execution'[1] and there are a number of factors that can influence whether staff convert their intention into action, or not. Identifying those actual practices of secure behaviour is a key element in why IS audit reviews are carried out. If audit only considers the policies, controls and procedures that exist, that gives very little information about how secure the general operations of

---

[1] Renaud and Goucher, 2014.

the organisation are. The auditor needs to identify whether these policies, controls and procedures are incorporated into day-to-day operations, and work with the organisation to recognise where action is required.

Let us now examine factors affecting the Gulf of Execution.

Management

A key factor is leadership by example and the encouragement of staff to work in a secure way. This may seem trivial when it does not necessarily involve formal training. However, a manager with a positive attitude to restrictions and controls, especially those that impact on normal working practice can make a big difference; for example, let us take a situation where a manager comes to work without their ID badge. This should be a problem, as access through the main door requires the badge to be swiped. This restriction not only provides protection for data and materials in the building, but it also provides protection in the event of fire because each worker's presence is recorded, and if they are not seen out of the building, firemen can go and try to find them. However, if the manager gets in through the fire escape door, courtesy of the smokers who stand outside having their cigarette break, he is showing a lack of respect to a process that protects him as well as data.

The positive attitude of an IS auditor in their dealings with managers can do much to encourage their positivity. They can do this by discussing security issues that managers have, especially where processes or controls seem to interfere with effective operations. As someone with a larger overall view of IS in the organisation, they may be able to help the manager and their staff find solutions, or raise the issue at a higher level so the issues can be addressed.

The availability of tools

An organisation may often have many staff working on tablets and laptops in public places, such as on planes or in cafes. Where this information might be personally or corporately sensitive, it may be agreed that they should take care of being 'shoulder surfed' or even having the screen image captured by CCTV or a smart phone. One way this risk can be mitigated is to use screen protectors, either physical or by software. However, if these are not readily available, for example, if the procurement process takes weeks rather than days, then the screens will go unprotected.

The IS auditor can, in a situation where the procurement process is causing problems, raise the issue in their report that will be read by senior managers who are in a position to review the process for security-critical items.

Operational effectiveness

Operational effectiveness of the controls is very much an issue that comes from the security team and weaknesses in this area are often due to a lack of communication. Someone who has been working in the area of IS for any length of time can develop a well-tuned sense of risk that readily identifies and is sceptical of new things that may lead to increased risk. The identification of the risk and the resulting secure behaviour can seem like 'common sense'. This means that the need to explain how and why to operate securely can seem so trivial as to be almost irritating to have to explain.

Looking at the effective operation of IS in an organisation is the core of the role of the IS auditor, so they need use their knowledge and experience to work with the organisation to ensure that their policies and controls are as effective as possible in normal operations, as well as in times of crisis. It is for the latter reason that elements such as the checking of the regular back-up and restoration process are important.

Training

I believe strongly in efficient, effective training. I suppose I should, as it is part of what I do. However, I have attended far too many training sessions that taught me little and used up time I desperately needed to spend doing my job. There are many approaches to training, some of which can even be delivered without PowerPoint! If there is an important point regarding required behaviour of an individual in the process of their job, then, in most cases, that message has to be 'sold' to them. It has to get their interest and their understanding of the requirement to change behaviour. Good training can make an important message about security seem common sense and straightforward, which can make the changes in the working process of staff more likely. I should also say that this link does overlap with the previous one to an extent because training should be designed with understanding both of the way staff carry out their work and the motivations that they bring to that operation. For example: for someone who works in a sales team, their motivation is likely to be getting the highest sales numbers, or value of sales, as possible, not least because that brings financial reward. It is therefore likely to be difficult to persuade them that security controls that get in the way of processing those sales, such as a policy not to use free WiFi provided in public places, is going to be unpopular, even if the need for it seems obvious to a technical person who is aware of the risk of interception of data on such a system. In this case, training needs to work with sales team motivations and requirements as much as possible, not condemn staff for holding them.

One of the responsibilities of the IS auditor is to consider how such controls or policies are likely to impact on normal operations, and therefore evaluate how likely they are to be consistently implemented. In the case of sales staff, for example, they might suggest that they are provided with high speed cellular connections so there is no need for them to use the WiFi at all.

POPULAR MISCONCEPTIONS ABOUT THE AUDIT ROLE

Through the course of this book I will be developing a picture of what an IS auditor does and how they can contribute to the operation and effectiveness of an organisation. However, it is important to recognise first that many take a number of negative ideas to their initial encounters with an auditor about how they will conduct their role. These may have been acquired from colleagues or based on past experience in other situations, but the origin is less important than the impact these ideas can have on the effectiveness of the relationship that will develop. It is important, therefore, for us to discuss some of the most common misconceptions before we go any further.

It is just about ticking boxes

There is no question that this is an approach that some auditors take, both in internal audit and in preparation for external certification. However, this approach makes the auditor nothing more than the 'checker of last resort', which is generally detrimental to the auditor as well as the business. **If the task is reduced to recognising compliance, the job becomes undervalued when compared with its potential**. After all, passively checking against prescribed rigid criteria removes the important active elements of analysis and input into the overall organisational process, so the level of skill and expertise required would be much less. Operating audit in such a way would bring the start of a downward spiral for auditors, because the less that is expected, the less their market value is, and then the less likely it is that good quality candidates are attracted. Indeed, if an audit task is reduced to this level it can make it very dull for the person carrying it out as there is no real challenge to retain their interest.

If the auditor is expected to be passive in their approach, then that reduces what is being checked to being perceived as either in place or not. There would be no room for evaluation of the effectiveness or operation.

A good auditor does not get involved with the business

This point develops from the last, but also comes from the attitude that requires the auditor not to turn over too many stones or find those areas of weakness that are currently difficult to address. If someone conducting an audit highlights a problem and potentially draws on the limited budget of the team, it can cause tension within the business unless it is understood that the auditor is there to help the organisation achieve compliance with the audit requirements.

It should be remembered that the very need for a compliance audit is business-driven. This is not an exercise that is undertaken lightly; it happens because it is necessary for the retention or development of the business.

A good audit role is one where the holder has the opportunity to use both their knowledge and experience of the business and of the standards which the business is using. As we will see later in this book, the challenge of maintaining current knowledge both of process and criteria, can be very challenging as it can require getting insight into forthcoming changes in external standards and understanding the impact of internal organisational changes on the assurance of secure practice.

Some people who are attracted to working in an internal audit team may be more comfortable with the contribution they can make with a good eye for detail and knowledge of internal systems, than the requirements of external accreditation demands. In larger organisations this may be entirely fine as there are plenty of internal process changes that need to be planned and checked. However, anyone aspiring to higher levels of IT and IS audit is going to need to utilise knowledge and experience, insight and communication skills to make the best contribution to the operation of the corporation.

This attitude also reflects a perception of the auditor as someone on the outside of operations, and therefore a 'common enemy'. From a social psychological approach, rallying a group together under the 'banner' of a common enemy can be an effective way to draw a team together. Those who draw satirical cartoons know that they need to find a 'face' or a person that the reader can identify as 'the enemy'. Look at the 'Walls have Ears' posters from the Second World War, and you will see the face of Adolf Hitler incorporated as the 'face of the enemy'. This tendency to personify the enemy means that, if audit requirements are believed to get in the way of normal operations or be excessively pedantic, the auditor who oversees implementation is potentially going to be seen as 'the enemy' and find themselves fighting against reluctant staff rather than working with them. So, far from being a statement about impartiality (on which more shortly), this is a statement highlighting a defensive reaction to the audit process. A key part of the IS auditor's role is to encourage and assist safer operation; they are much less likely to be able to do that if they are seen as an 'enemy'. Wherever this attitude is found, work needs to be done to prepare those involved for a more positive audit experience. This can often be achieved by helping them to appreciate the audit role and the benefits it brings to a business.

However, this is only part of the potential difficulties arising from this misconception. While the mind-set of those being audited is important, so too is the attitude of the auditors themselves. An effective auditor should be sensitive and flexible in approach when working with the operational areas in a way that gains as much co-operation as possible. Research in the area of developing a positive security culture, such as by Goo, Yim and Kim[2] emphasises the importance of audit being seen as a positive aspect of the process of secure operation.

A good auditor maintains the 'status quo' where possible

When I gathered the opinions of some experienced IS auditors, this misconception was amongst the ideas mentioned. This really concerns pressure that can be put on internal auditors not to 'rock the boat' by finding issues that are not obvious. Once a report raises a significant issue, then senior management, and probably the board, are deemed to know about the problem and are responsible for seeing that it is either rectified or formally accepted as a risk. From this logically comes the idea that a good auditor tries to maintain the status quo, and thereby not cost the business in time and other investment. If the person conducting the audit is too junior to have any power to make suggestions at a level that will get reasonable consideration,

---

[2] Goo et al., 2013.

and is not sufficiently supported to be able to discuss the issue within their team or with their line manager, they may not feel able to confront a problematic issue and will thereby ignore it. This problem can also arise if the audit is conducted internally and the auditor role is just one part of their job description. They may be unwilling to confront difficult issues that may harm the relationship with the colleagues they work alongside in the rest of their working week. However, there can be a fine line between 'giving the benefit of the doubt' and allowing the system being audited to stagnate. To avoid this, a good auditor (of which more later) needs to strengthen their position by keeping ahead of the game in terms of understanding IT and IS developments and changes in risk. This gives greater credibility if they are in a position where they need to suggest the need for operational changes. While this may not be easy news to receive, not least because there may not be any obviously simple solutions to the change in risk, the auditor needs to be able to draw attention to those areas that require, or will soon require, significant consideration.

A good example of this has been the fast emergence of the use of tablet devices in the business context. These first came to market during an economic slump, this meant that businesses had to look at the added value that investment in the devices might bring as what they did was not very different from a laptop, only in a smaller and easier to manage package. At a time of squeezed budgets, many organisations felt they could not justify their purchase. However, as has already been said, their convenience, and utility as a leisure device, meant that many were bought privately, and often used for work during commuting and other business travel; the BYOD phenomenon. Understandably, the potential of having sensitive business information flowing through devices over which the organisation has no control causes concern. Indeed, some organisations have been trying to understand how they can control and influence, at the very least, the antivirus protection and the privacy settings on these devices. However, the question is how this can be done when the software cannot be installed and monitored from the main system – the standard method with the previous generation of mobile devices, the laptop. The extent of this challenge may be more apparent to the internal auditor, who is aware of the use, and potentially some of the problems, this has caused. They are then in a position to identify that in an audit so that these issues can be considered before there is a security incident, especially where there is significant use of non-corporate devices within the organisation. In a case such as this, an auditor may serve their organisation well in helping to push against the status quo in terms of staff use and see how any risk can be better understood and potentially managed. However, where the risk is being downplayed in order to avoid the need for investment, raising issues may be unpopular.

While all organisations have to keep an eye on their budgets and act responsibly to that end, they have a specific responsibility to keep sensitive information safe. Given the growing financial and reputational damage that IS failures can bring, it is important that IS auditors feel themselves able to identify weaknesses as well as strengths. Dealing with the issues can lead to investment of a greater order than expected, but the penalties can also cause unwelcome problems. That is a decision that is not the auditor's to make, even where they are an internal auditor. They have to present their findings and recommendations and leave that problem to those higher up the hierarchy.

So far we have looked at what the IS audit role includes and the misconceptions sometimes held that can get in the way of getting maximum benefit from an IS audit.

If you are new to IS auditing, or considering it as a career move, these insights are useful, but you really need to know if you have what it takes to be good at the job. In the next section I am going to help you to answer that.

BUILDING A MODEL INFORMATION SECURITY AUDITOR

Having considered some of the misconceptions regarding the work of IS auditors, which audit professionals themselves believe get in the way of good practice, I felt that a useful approach might be to devise a 'model' auditor.

I must put a caveat in before I start. I studied economics (amongst a few other things) at university and one of the first things we were told about modelling a situation is that it is a combination of ideals; it is not about duplicating or mirroring reality.[3] So if you are looking to recruit or develop an IS auditor, do not expect to find a single embodiment of all the skills and attributes below; and if such a person exists you probably can't afford them.

For the purpose of this model I have divided the required elements into attributes and skills. Attributes are aspects of the personality or normal behaviour of a person, whereas skills are learnt. Skills generally comprise knowledge and experience acquired through training and doing relevant work, which is then expressed in action. Of course, things are rarely as cut and dried as the 'either-or' elements I list below and 'attributes' can be further developed, just like skills. For example, some people are fundamentally good communicators, able to explain their opinion in a clear and concise way. However, practice and experience will help them to become familiar with the way their approach may need to be adjusted to different environments and situations. Of course, where someone does not have a basic attribute as part of their core personality this just means they have to work to learn and develop that skill.

ATTRIBUTES OF A MODEL IS AUDITOR

- a systematic approach to work;
- intellectual curiosity;
- a good communicator;
- patience and a high boredom threshold;
- an eye for detail;
- strong character;

---

[3] This could be the opinion of my economics lecturer, rather than an 'official' definition of an economics model, but in any case it does explain why economic models often seem to bear little resemblance to the 'real world'.

41

- a politically sensitive approach;
- flexibility;
- tendency towards professional scepticism.

Some of these are more obvious than others so let us go through each in turn and examine what they mean and why they are important.

A systematic approach to work

By this attribute I do not mean that an auditor needs to be a 'towel straightener' with a compulsive attitude to neatness. I mean that their approach needs to be consistent and repeatable and therefore more likely to be able to be demonstrated as fair.

The negative manifestation of a systems-driven personality is what is sometimes known as a 'job's worth'; that is, someone who rigidly adheres to rules. Our model auditor is not like that. They will understand the rules, but be able to take a dispassionate view and find ways for the requirements to meet operational need.

Our model auditor will look at process and guidelines and compare those to the requirements of the standard which the organisation is being audited to or against. I make this differentiation because some organisations may audit *against* a standard, in that they have no requirement to conform currently, but believe either that it is something they should be working towards or that they can use it as a guideline to implement more operationally secure practices. In contrast, when an organisation is being audited *to* a standard it is required to meet whatever criteria are stipulated.

It is important to appreciate that there are all sorts of pressures, both internal and external, around an audit situation, and it is very important that the question of why the audit is taking place is appreciated at the beginning of the process. This is important for a number of reasons. For example, if the need to achieve compliance is driven from a key customer requirement, then senior or board level pressure may be exerted for the auditor to recognise compliance with minimum disruption and the greatest haste. In this case, the auditor needs to approach the work pragmatically and systematically in order that certification can be achieved smoothly. If the auditor is focused on the guidelines that they are assessing against, rather than becoming involved with internal politics or considering how to deal with strong personalities, it makes it more straightforward to demonstrate compliance as well as areas of concern. It is like having to show all your 'working out' when doing maths at school. The answer, in this case the result of the audit, is the same, but it is easier for the organisation to see the reasons behind the decision, and areas they need to address in the short or medium term.

The ability to focus on achieving the task in hand while appreciating operational requirements and restrictions can be one of the hardest aspects of the role of an internal auditor. As employees of the same organisation, they have the same overall organisational objectives as those being audited. Also, an internal auditor may be concerned that they want to maintain good working relationships with colleagues beyond the audit. For example, if the internal audit is to provide a key customer with reassurance that information is processed in a secure manner, it is in the interest of all staff, including the internal auditor, that this assurance is given in order to help to secure existing business and even bring new business.

It is in this sort of situation that having a systematic approach can help the auditor to keep their focus on the task and, if not ignore, at least have less concern for the internal issues that can be a distraction. It is worth remembering that if the internal auditor's conclusion is not upheld by a subsequent external audit then that can cause more problems than initially overlooking, or underplaying, an issue solved.

A good internal auditor withstands internal pressure to judge marginal issues in favour of the organisation and takes a systematic approach, thereby giving an opinion of the practice of IS in the organisation that can be trusted.

Intellectual curiosity

It might appear to the outsider that an auditor needs only to understand the standards that they are measuring against. Why, if they generally only assess compliance to PCIDSS (The Payment Card Industry Data Security Standard, which is a standard to protect sensitive customer information when processing card payments) does an auditor need to understand the requirements of, for example, ISO 22301 (the standard for business continuity)?

There are a number of reasons, including external requirements from customers, why it would be wise for an auditor to ensure that they are familiar, at least in general terms, with standards their customers are likely to have to be compliant with in order to be able to respond to queries and to ensure that none of their practices contravenes any requirements.

It is important, therefore, for an auditor to be sufficiently self-driven to keep up with new trends, both in business and in technology. Indeed, they need to be looking out for new threats. For example, the way that business is able to be conducted makes it easier than ever to work away from the formal office setting. This can lead to challenges in risk from things such as the increased use of cloud-based storage, especially non-corporate clouds like Google Drive. In many cases, staff may use these kinds of private utilities without being aware of the risks to which they are exposing their business.

There are also challenges that come from the big change in ownership, and power over devices that people work on. Until very recently, businesses were able to restrict access to their systems to those computers that they owned and managed. This meant that they could be assured, and assure any compliance auditor, of their security update procedure and such like. Now, staff can often access a great deal of their company work from devices they own themselves. This has legal repercussions in terms of the ability of the employing organisation to have control of the technical security. Also, wearable devices, led by Google Glass, are fast approaching the wider market. What will the position of organisations be with regard to such devices and their use? **The day the first one arrives on the premises is too late to decide policy**.

The IS auditor needs to ask these sorts of questions now and encourage businesses to prepare themselves; however, to do that they need to understand the devices, their threat and capability and the potential impact of any emerging threat. Of course, not all new developments threaten IS – it is arguable that the ability to read documents on glasses would make them less vulnerable to shoulder surfing in a public place, for example.

With these sorts of issues on the horizon, and no generally agreed 'fix' available, our model auditor needs to be aware of the overall threat landscape and any significant competing ideas and opinions surrounding it. These can be gained by reading appropriate industry publications, attending conferences and other events, even joining online forums and discussions where such issues are aired, especially where the perspective is audit.

A good communicator

As I mentioned earlier in this book, a key responsibility of the IS auditor is to enhance the operations of an organisation. However, this is not generally appreciated, so the auditor needs to interact effectively in order to overcome, or at least reduce, any negative attitudes. There is a lot that can be learnt about communicating, and I will discuss this later when looking at skills, but having a good appreciation of what good communication is like will help those skills to develop.

Good communication results in both the transmitter and the receiver of information understanding the information in a similar way. Mistakes can happen where understanding is assumed or where the transmitting person makes insufficient effort to consider how their message might be received by someone with different experiences or perspectives.

On 26 August 2014 the Information Commissioners Office (ICO) issued a statement about an incident of repeated leakage of highly sensitive information by the Ministry of Justice. The second incident occurred because, as a result of an earlier incident, prisons in England and Wales were supplied with back-up discs that were capable of being encrypted. Unfortunately it appears that those receiving access to the discs were not told that the encryption was set to Off as default and needed to be turned on to operate as required. In his statement, ICO Head of Enforcement, Stephen Eckersley, said: 'The fact that a government department with security oversight for prisons can supply equipment to 75 prisons throughout England and Wales without properly understanding, let alone telling them, how to use it beggars belief.'[4]

There are two particular reasons why an IS auditor needs to be able to communicate well from the very beginning of their career. First is because of the nature of audit; it is most likely that an auditor will be talking to people at a higher level in the hierarchy than they might otherwise expect to do if they also hold a non-audit role. It is important, therefore, that our model auditor must not be daunted by presenting their opinions and ideas at a senior level. Senior managers are generally very busy people looking for efficient, effective communication and that is best achieved with knowledge and confidence. At the same time, the IS auditor has to be careful not to come across in an arrogant or self-promoting way that will take the focus away from the task in hand.

Second, ensuring compliance with internal or external requirements can often be challenging because of the way they are written. Almost all audit requirements, certainly the external ones, are designed to avoid ambiguity where possible and this often leads to the use of more complex language and

---

[4] ICO statement 26 August 2014. http://ico.org.uk/news/latest_news/2014/repeated-security-failings-lead-to-180000-fine-for-moj-26082014 [accessed 26 August 2014].

prescribed approaches that can be hard to equate with the operational situation in which they are to be applied.

If the auditor is internally employed, their task can be made more challenging by having to perform this complex translation while being mindful of organisational culture and sensitive political issues. After all, they are employed by the organisation and need to maintain a good relationship with colleagues after the audit is complete. One example of a tricky situation could be that a new auditor finds that the previous internal audit missed a significant, and obvious, weakness in the change control process and that audit was carried out by the head of internal audit, who is the new auditor's boss. The new auditor needs to be able to communicate clearly, but sensitively, about the problem and any repercussions arising from the oversight while continuing to build a good relationship with their colleagues and especially their boss.

Effective communication is not just a two dimensional thing between the sender and receiver. There are levels of trust and understanding that build around it and make working together smoother and possibly easier. Understanding this is even more important when one considers that the auditor is not a checklist operative. They are generally not just looking to check compliance against a rigid set of controls or requirements (except, arguably, in the case of PCIDSS). They are looking for policies and controls that meet compliance objectives in a way that is operationally sound for the organisation. They are working with the business to link operational need and compliance objectives. This means they need the trust and co-operation of the staff to be effective.

Communication works more than one way. There is the way that the auditor communicates with others in order to explain matters, such as in the example above. They also need to be aware of the way information regarding operational problems and potential incidents is received, and how it is efficiently and effectively dealt with. In order for this information to be communicated, staff must feel able to report issues without fear for their job stability or career progression. If that is not the case then significant situations leading to security weaknesses may continue for too long.

Let us consider the common problem of a staff member who thinks they have lost their mobile device. If they think they may get into trouble with their boss, they are less likely to inform the IS team. They may wait several hours, or even days, until all hope that they have put it down and forgotten where is lost. This makes it harder for the security team to take effective mitigating action, as the device may already have been compromised and data accessed. This, of course, is compounded when the user owns the device themselves (BYOD). The organisation may never be officially informed of the potential compromise. This is a difficult situation because staff with corporate devices are generally encouraged to take care of them by the threat of disciplinary action following a loss. However, use of mobile devices is widespread so it is a matter that needs to be addressed. The auditor needs to be assured that the communication of the process of reporting of lost devices is clear and functional.

Patience and a high boredom threshold

Maybe this is something that I should not list as a useful attribute of an IS auditor in a book about audit and its appeal as a career, but I think we have to be honest: there are times when the business of working through policies and compliance documentation can be less than exciting. When a new standard is published, the auditor needs not only to read it, but also to make sure that they understand it and recognise changes from previous versions, especially where they directly concern their own organisation as well as other organisations they may audit. This is not, generally, interesting work. But it is very necessary.

Also, auditors often have to read policy documents as well as attend meetings about policies and processes. It is true that many business meetings, can be dull, but having a meeting to discuss policies, how they work or how they need to change, can be challenging. Especially if the auditor is external to the organisation, so should be working in a supportive role as they work out problems rather than making decisions themselves. Having to deal with less challenging work from time to time can provide opportunities to catch up on current issues or training, and this is where the IS auditor's ability to keep themselves engaged through the more mundane aspects of the job is a great benefit. Indeed, having a strategy for keeping yourself engaged during dull work is probably a good skill to develop in a lot of corporate life. Sometimes an IS audit can seem straightforward. If an organisation is one that has a clear need to protect information, such as one working with the defence sector, it may have well-established, appropriate procedures in place rather than requiring design and implementation of new processes from the beginning.

This means that, as an external auditor working in such a formally controlled sector, there are many factors that repeat across a number of organisations. The work can become routine, but being able to retain interest is essential because otherwise slight differences might be missed.

Eye for detail

The ideal auditor will get satisfaction in work from their eye for detail and their ability to solve problems. Systems constantly evolve and the demands made on them are also changing. Standards and requirements, by their nature, are very unlikely to be in place before some or all of the organisations affected have already had to make adjustments and changes. A good auditor will often identify where changes may lead to the need for action or consideration of future action. These changes may be small, but if they are identified before any incident results this is a big benefit for the organisation as a whole.

Having an eye for detail is important in this sort of situation as it can be difficult to identify trends and opinions of industry leaders and so pick up on the likely changes. Often the information is subtle and easy to miss, so the ability to carefully process information for the pertinent detail is a real benefit. To be able to do this, the ideal auditor needs to monitor appropriate online information, discussions, webinars and the like as well as attend briefing and conference events.

Of course, having a concern for the precision of detail can also be very useful in the case of existing standards where strict adherence is required. In the vast amount of documentation that can be generated in the preparation to any certification, it can be easy to miss a detail that the accreditor or external auditor finds problematic.

These are the sort of things that are likely to be overlooked by someone who has less affinity with detail. Basically, what makes a model auditor comes from their interest in the detail of documentation as well as implementation. As with many of these attributes, an eye for detail can be developed through adding skill that comes from experience and hard work. However, having an eye for detail as a basic part of one's personality just makes that learning a lot easier.

Strength of character

It is necessary for an auditor to be able to hold their ground, especially when working in an internal audit team where, as discussed in Chapter 1, the pressures may be higher. It can be very tempting, in particular for a newer, less experienced auditor, to go with a 'status quo' approach as it can be very difficult to argue for the need to invest in technology or education, especially when budgets are tight and where it had been hoped that the existing system would be sufficient. However, as business processes develop so must secure processes. It is important that the internal auditor be willing to be unpopular in the bringing of expensive news. While an external auditor may have to bring the same sort of news, the implications of that news are less personal because it does not affect their own organisation directly.

Some of the most common security weaknesses in established organisations are in their legacy systems; that is, systems that have been built around and incorporated past the point where they are supported by patches or have their access controls monitored. I once attended a very interesting talk by Peter Woods, a well-known White Hat consultant, to a group of public sector staff who had some responsibility for security. He explained that many passwords on legacy systems are often still set at the factory default settings such as 1234 or 'admin', which made them vulnerable to relatively low skill external attack or hack. At the next break there were quite a few very intense calls back to IT departments to pass on the news. As the departments and the systems grew, the awareness of the problem of legacy systems and their protection had been lost.

The approach and knowledge base of the auditor will go a long way to forming a productive relationship with organisations, or areas within organisations. Fundamentally the auditor must know what they are doing. If they have kept their knowledge of both the elements of the audit and the requirements of accreditation bodies up to date then they can provide the most effective assistance to the staff involved in the audit. It is also important that the auditor tries to establish a spirit of co-operation with those being audited. This can enable small issues to be highlighted and dealt with before they become significant in being recorded in the final report. Having the strength of character required to carry out effective audits can be difficult, but it is much more so if the auditor is on the defensive as a result of their weak knowledge.

A politically sensitive approach

One of the hardest, but most rewarding, parts of the role of auditor, whether internal or external, is working with people to improve and maintain an effective approach to security. This can sometimes mean that bad news, with regard to particular areas of implementation, needs to be communicated in a helpful way and with due sensitivity for the internal political context. So, for example, there may be areas of weakness resulting from budget decisions taken higher up the hierarchy than the staff the auditor is working with. Care needs to be taken to work within those constraints while, where appropriate, drawing attention in the final report to any critical issues that need further discussion at more senior levels.

Flexibility

This is another description that may surprise people about an auditor. Surely audit is about rigidity? That is certainly true, especially in terms of fairness and pragmatism. However, in most cases[5] those who devise guidelines for standards are aware that there are, by necessity, operational differences between the various organisations. For example, a small company specialising in forensic analysis of computers would not require the complexity of policies, procedures and guidelines that a major petrochemical company would, so there has to be operational flexibility in the interpretation and application of guidelines.

Being both consistent and flexible is a tough ask of anyone and requires sound knowledge and experience. It has to be said that the requirement for flexibility can be frustrating for the auditor. For example, a risk assessment may be carried out and a risk may be accepted at board level that the auditor feels would have been best acted on. However, as long as there is justification as well as acceptance, and this is expressed in a way that will be acceptable to any external audit or review, then an auditor has to be prepared to accept that. Of course an external assessor may have more power to suggest strongly that the issue is addressed, but even they may have to go along with the decision of the board to allow risk.

---

[5] PCIDSS being a notable exception to this.

Tendency towards professional scepticism

Suggesting that professional scepticism is a useful attribute for an IS auditor is not the same as saying that they should be naturally distrustful. Rather, it means that they need to look for evidence to support claims both of compliance or non-compliance because any evidence presented to an external auditor needs to be supported.

In the Requirements and Security Assessment Procedures for PCIDSS[6] each requirement is presented with recommended testing procedures. Universal use of these assures consistency between certifications of the level that is required by the ethos of the standard. While other standards are less rigid, it is still important that the supporting evidence is persuasive.

This is especially important where the initial pre-audit is carried out internally, but will ultimately be subject to external scrutiny. An internal auditor may know something to be true by their personal knowledge, or trust the person asserting the truth of the statement, but neither of these factors is sufficient for an external auditor. It is much better that the internal auditor takes a sceptical approach and requires sound evidence to support any claims that are being made.

Some internal auditors who have to learn to be sceptical can feel uncomfortable because their colleagues might see their demands as a sign of distrust rather than a way of ensuring that statements given to an external auditor are accepted.

SKILLS REQUIRED OF A MODEL IS AUDITOR

Having looked at the attributes that comprise our ideal model IS auditor, the next stage is to consider the skills, some built on attributes, that will help to develop the model. One of the interesting conundrums that I have been challenged with as I

---

[6] PCIDSS Requirements and Security Assessment Procedures Version 3.0, November 2013.

write this section is asking myself Is this a skill? What is a skill anyway? I am defining a skill as the learning or ability linked to practical application. For example, being able to stand up to give a good presentation is arguably something most people can do, as long as they can express themselves in a way their audience understands. However, many presenters who believe they have always had that aptitude still get some help in their early days. In fact I would argue that a good presenter learns from every talk they watch, as well as those they give. So they may have a good aptitude, but then build their skills continuously.

In this section I am including skills that all auditors, internal or external, need to develop from the earliest stage in their engagement in the role. It is important to understand what these might be and why they are important because it is likely that those considering an audit role, or already in one as a novice, will need training and guided experience to learn or develop the skills. It can be expected that all of these skills will be developed further as the auditor progresses in their career.

It should also be noted that in all of the elements I have listed below, skill needs experience to anchor it down. My dad is a carpenter; I know he is because he has a certificate saying that he qualified. Nobody would have employed him without proof that he had a certain level of skill. However, the experience he gathered in his work career means that his skills are still relevant and useful more than 50 years later.

Skills of a model IS auditor:

- communication;
- knowledge of IT systems and architectural principles;
- a solid understanding of compliance and regulatory standards;
- analytical, critical and strategic thinking;
- an understanding of the risk process;
- managing personal development;
- ability to work autonomously;

- managing time effectively;
- project management;
- an understanding of change management;
- a good understanding of data analytics;
- an awareness of the spiky nature of laurels;
- making every effort to maintain awareness of both change and expected change to relevant legislation and regulation impacts.

Communication skills

While previously I have identified good communication as an attribute, a part of an auditor's personality, for some it is not. Some need to learn to communicate effectively, and for them it is a skill. Indeed, even those who have communication as an attribute need to continually develop it as a skill. Communication skills refer to the ability to gather information. That is an essential ability that anyone joining or progressing in the profession needs. Attending a meeting with full attention can be much harder than we expect, especially when the overall tone is somewhat dull and the content to be covered means that the meeting is long, or if it is an interview format where every moment needs full concentration. The auditor needs to make sure they do not miss any important things that are said. That is not because they want to find fault or catch people out; if there is an area of weakness then, especially if the audit is internal, they need to get involved in helping to find a solution.

Listening skills

As G.K. Chesterton said: 'There's a lot of difference between listening and hearing.'

We may monitor the information being given to us by a colleague, but actually be concentrating on something else. In a meeting situation, when the item being discussed is of little relevance to you, it is easy to slip into this approach. So listening, that is, receiving the transmitted verbal data and processing it in the context of the discussion, is not as easy as it seems.

Common listening mistakes include:

- Not concentrating on the information, just monitoring for key words or phrases that are of interest – if you will not admit to doing this at work, maybe you will accept you have done it with family or friends.

- Listening to a discussion primarily in order to find where you can next speak. I have never found anyone who will admit to doing this, but I have seen it happen often.

- Seeing a discussion as a battle that must be won and therefore listening for weaknesses in every point that can be challenged. This is a 'levelled up' version of the previous point, where listening is really secondary to speaking. This situation may be absorbing for those immediately involved, but can make it difficult to keep to an agreed agenda and can be less satisfactory for others in the room to witness.

- Allowing distractions to take your focus away from the discussion. Phones and computers contribute to this as they make it even easier to slip into the situation of monitoring rather than listening.

- A lack of respect for the opinion of other parties is a critical element in most of the points above. In any conversation it is important to allow all participants to feel their opinion is valued and respected.

- Only listening to what is said. Ernest Hemingway said: 'When people talk, listen completely. Most people never listen.' If you listen to people, it is at least as important to listen to what they are *not* saying as to what they are saying. So, for example, if you ask them a question is that question answered fully or is the answer subtly evasive? This is particularly important in an audit situation: most people will try and avoid lying to an auditor, but they may take care in the choice of their words to withhold or deflect from facts they would prefer not to share. Developing the skill of listening to the spoken and unspoken word makes for the most effective of listeners.

Interview skills

In the context of the development of an IS auditor, interviews can be used in a number of different ways. An internal audit interview is about information gathering and forging a working relationship. Interview skills need a wide range of elements of communication. Perhaps the most obvious is to ask questions that invite the interviewee to open up and give the interviewer more information than they had when the interview started. This means using open questions that require more detail than a straightforward yes or no answer. Some interviewers seem to have learnt their interview approach from crime shows, and so feel they need to trip someone up and get them to admit a problem or weakness that was otherwise hard to find. This is not a good idea. An auditor using a combative approach undermines any other efforts they make to give the impression of the audit being helpful to staff, so questioning works best when most of it gives scope for a more open reply.

Then the interviewer needs to be able to take in all the information that the interviewee is giving them in their approach and answers. They need to listen to what is being said; are there conditional phrases being used such as 'in an ideal world', or 'I would like to be able to'. These can show that the interviewee understands what is required, even if, for whatever reason, they are unable to deliver. Listening well makes it easier to put follow-up questions that flow with the discussion of the individuals, not following a set pattern. Also the interviewer can possibly detect subjects that the interviewee is trying not to talk about, possibly tasks they know they should have seen done, but have been overlooked. Sometimes it is enough to detect that and note it. Pushing a point can make the interview seem more like a grilling than a discussion that aims to lead to the improvement of security in the organisation. In most cases, if the interviewee feels as if the interviewer is picking up subtle points and pushing forward to find more, it is likely that they will say as little as they feel that they can get away with.

The next stage in interview communication is feeding back; that is, the interviewer giving their interpretation or view on something said. Generally speaking, most people will give more information if the feedback is reasonably positive. For example, the auditor might say: 'From what you say, you seem to have been putting a lot of effort into improving the security of data in the organisation. What would you say is your biggest current challenge?' This is asking the interviewee what is still not working well, but doing that in a way that acknowledges their work so far. It is also asking for their opinion, and that is quite respectful, which people generally respond well to. Of course, if the interviewee has painted a bleak view of the current state of things, the skilled interviewer will not contradict, but guide the discussion to try and reveal the root concern behind their opinion. It might even be that their real concern is a clash of personalities between themselves and their line manager. There may not actually be a problem that is relevant to the audit and that needs to be established or it can add confusion with the information finally gathered.

On the other hand, using an approach that leaves the interviewee feeling like they were never seriously challenged or the weak areas of their security were not identified at all does not promote the role of IS audit either. So, using the full range of communication skills is vital to getting the most out of any interview, for both sides.

Note-taking skills

Note-taking skills face a similar challenge to listening skills, as notes need to be taken to ensure nothing is missed. Exactly what 'note-taking' means can vary. I once had a college lecturer who insisted that his words of wisdom were taken down verbatim. This meant that we did not really listen to his words, we were focused on getting it all down. In fact, as he read his lecture directly from his prepared script, he could have saved a lot of time by just copying his notes, handing them to students and therefore cutting out the lecture stage altogether. When auditors are interviewing, in a meeting or even on a phone call, there may be information that needs to be carefully recorded as close to word-for-word as possible, but mostly it is information that is needed, not the script. It is best to say that notes should be accurate and clear. If it is important that the information being recorded is precise, reading it back to the other parties so they can agree with the wording used may be appropriate. Where information is not recorded, issues might be missed or assistance that was offered is not then delivered. Developing the skill to take accurate notes is therefore very important. Where someone is not confident in their skill it is worth arranging for someone else to take notes at the same time, and then any differences can be discussed later and confidence can be built.

In most circumstances the medium used to take notes is not important. I still tend to take hand written notes (or personally encrypted scribbles, as my husband describes them) and then write or type them up as soon as possible later. My children, however, who are both 'Screenagers', can type as fast as I can speak while still chatting. They have grown up with a keyboard at their fingertips and, like many of their generation, typing fast is more natural to them.

There may, however, be situations where taking digital notes could be counter-productive. If the discussion is informal the other party may well be very uncomfortable having their words recorded in front of them. In those circumstances, if it is appropriate to make a note at all, it should be made as soon afterwards as possible and stored with due consideration of the discretion needed.

Experience has taught me that it is also important for those taking notes to be sensitive as to what to include and what to leave out; for example, a discussion may become heated and personal remarks might be made. While the subject being discussed probably does need to be recorded, recording things said in the passion of the moment is unlikely to serve any useful purpose. It is very unlikely to be useful to an auditor.

I should add that in internal meetings and interviews the level of detail in notes is often covered by culture and practice within that organisation. In that situation the note-taker should follow the general practice unless there is a good reason for not doing so. Providing attendees with an eight-page verbatim account of a meeting, when general practice in the organisation is for the minutes to note key facts, important points made and action points ascribed, is likely to annoy them with the extra reading. They may also be more circumspect about making any objections to a point as they know this will be entirely recorded.

It is important to keep in mind that audit notes may be very sensitive, particularly in relation to architecture or internal politics, and their storage and transmission should be carefully considered.

Knowledge of IT systems and architectural principles

One auditor who responded to my question about required skills said that an IS auditor needs 'less IT knowledge than you might think'. This is not, however, the same as not needing any.

As IS is generally part of, or an offshoot of, the IT team in most organisations, there is an expectation that an IS person will have spent some of their career or training working with computers in a fairly complex way. However, as organisations gradually spread responsibility for IS implementation to include operational and managerial areas, it is possible that an increasing range of people who have experience of being responsible for some of IS will not have a background in IT. While auditors need to understand IT systems as they relate to security and operations, they do not need to be able to design and build them themselves. However, they need enough knowledge to interpret information they are given, such as the results of a penetration test. This needs to be learnt, like most other skills, and kept up to date. For some, gaining enough understanding and skill to be able to audit an organisation and its IT system confidently may be a challenge. A good method of meeting that challenge may be to allow the trainee auditor to access appropriate training, and possibly giving them a more IT knowledgeable mentor who can answer queries and guide them as they develop their IT skills.

While an auditor needs plenty of knowledge, practical experience (especially of the stricter demands of technical compliance) is one of the most important elements in the development of a junior auditor. If that auditor does not have such skills and experience then it is particularly important for them to be involved in technical audits so they can learn those skills and gather the experience they need.

Our model auditor will have the skills to understand the technical elements of their audits, and be able to help to find solutions to issues that may arise.

A solid understanding of compliance and regulatory standards

You might think that it is a given for an IS auditor to have an understanding of the various compliance and regulatory standards against which to audit, but actually it is less common than you might think. As skill in understanding and imparting knowledge of compliance and regulatory standards does not come naturally to people it needs to be learnt and updated regularly.

Some IS auditors reduce their workload by staying focused on the standards that they work with routinely rather than widening their understanding. While this is understandable where the auditor is very busy with current work, it can mean that new issues relating to areas they have little knowledge of can arise without warning; for example, the general trend for organisations and private individuals to outsource storage to cloud facilities and the impact of BYOD was anticipated by some, but other organisations have found they are pressured to catch up with the challenges of data management with documents moving to BYOD devices and, potentially, to private clouds. Those internal auditors who were aware of the growing discussion of these challenges over the last few years have been able to better advise their organisation to keep ahead of many others in terms of security of data.

Standards cannot be changed as often or as quickly as technology changes, so an auditor needs to understand the principles and requirements of the standards to be able to have a rational discussion with the accreditor or external auditor regarding any areas at issue.

INFORMATION SECURITY AUDITOR

Regulation changes are always a tricky time for an auditor. In 2013/14, after a period of reasonable stability, new versions of PCIDSS, ISO/IEC 27001 and SPF were issued. Talk about the spacing of buses! In this case, although there is a period of overlap with most standards during which time those approaching external audit to the previous standard or regulations can continue, preparations should look forward to the shape and content of the new standard if possible. It is therefore helpful for IS auditors, and others giving relevant advice, to be aware of the probable nature of any significant changes. This means that if an organisation is making any significant changes to organisational controls or processes, they can consider the likely incoming requirements.

It is in development periods for new regulation that professional networking, and attending appropriate industry events, has the potential to pay off. When ISO/IEC 27001:2013 was in development I was keen to try and get some insight into its likely form. Of course, during that stage there were no formal presentations or seminars that told me what to expect. However, I was fortunate to know someone who was involved in the process and, while he could not tell me what the new standard was going to be like, I came away from our discussion with the strong impression that the active involvement of middle as well as senior level management was of concern. I was able to ensure that training I developed in the meantime emphasised the need for wider responsibility for security beyond the IT department and the board level. When the standard was published that was a key change and I was glad that I had been able to guide clients to that mind-set early.

Analytical, critical and strategic thinking

This is another element that may be an attribute some have, but others need to learn. Like other skills, experience that can be gained will anchor and strengthen it. Some junior audit staff will have the background, personality or both that gives them confidence in critical thinking and good analytical skills from quite an early stage while others will need the opportunity to develop them.

The ability to look at an issue analytically in order to understand its purpose and function is vital to someone working in audit. They have to look at risk and understand solutions and proposed solutions in the context of external and internal requirements. They need to be able to do so critically, so the solution can be evaluated in terms of effectiveness, and strategically, so the solution can be understood for how its design and operation fit with the strategic goals of the organisation.

It can be difficult for any junior staff, not just audit staff, to gain enough insight into the wider operation of an organisation to be able to develop their strategic skills. Strategic thinking is a skill that can be a challenge for some as it requires the opportunity to learn and gain experience in decision making at a strategic level. In some organisations this sort of opportunity is not commonly available for junior staff. However, in the audit area it is necessary to give trainee staff as much supported experience as possible.

Our model auditor will be good at analytical thinking, but even they need to have the opportunity to exercise that skill, and learn how to communicate their ideas in an appropriate way.

An understanding of the risk process

The process of encouraging secure operations starts with the identification of risk. This might seem straightforward; you either understand it or you do not. Indeed, you may be wondering why I have listed the understanding of risk as a skill at all. Is it understanding linked to practical application? I would argue that it certainly is. It is possible to recognise a business risk, but the risk process means that this recognition is understood in the context of the operational environment of the business an auditor is working with. Risk can be very subjective between different situations. Indeed, one of the important reasons why security awareness does not transfer to 100 per cent secure behaviour is that in many cases, while staff accept something as a risk to IS, it may not seem like a risk that is relevant to their work situation. A skilled practitioner will be able to identify those risks that are relevant in the operation of the organisation they are dealing with. The identification of risk can be raised when preparing the organisation for an audit to standards set by an external standard, such as ISO 27000, or standards used by a significant customer or other stakeholder.

Once identified, the risk, and any remedial action that is required to deal with it, must be considered in the wider context of the operation of the organisation. A change in one area may have significant effects on others. For example, a commonly recognised risk for many organisations is the concern of data loss resulting from a member of staff copying sensitive information onto a USB stick and then losing it. There were many examples of such incidents in 2008 in the mainstream press, and now many organisations have a policy that states that information can only be copied onto encrypted USB sticks. Providing there are sticks available at short notice this is unlikely to cause too many issues for people who work in a physical office. However, where staff are mobile there can be problems regarding the availability of encrypted USBs and even the ease by which documents can be downloaded from a secure connection. Anything that makes it more difficult to operate can deter people. If the change only affects a few staff it is possible this difficultly will not be recognised soon enough and staff may find a work-around.

In 2009 I was analysing data from interview of some people who worked in an NHS trust about IS. As a result of all the publicity, their governing body had directed that sensitive information could only be transferred using an encrypted USB stick. However, the lead-time on the procurement of these sticks was counted in weeks or months rather than in days. One member of staff had the job of visiting GP practices to talk about identifying potential abuse in their patients. As part of the talk there were a series of pictures showing physical abuse. This member of staff could not be given an encrypted laptop because she only gave a few such talks in a year. She had a similar problem in getting a USB stick. In the end, the only way she could get the pictures to the GP practices was to send them via email. The staff member was appalled at this as it meant that images had to be downloaded at the practices and so were legitimately on a computer there. So, instead of the images being safe on one machine or USB stick, they were all across the town within a year.

Where the risk is of significant concern, an auditor will want to satisfy themselves that either the risk is small, and the appropriate person or people are willing to accept that there is a risk, or that the risk is so small that mitigating it will be more problematic than is justified. ISO/IEC 27001(2013) makes it clear that those who are recorded as having responsibility over a risk must be able to demonstrate awareness of the implications of that risk. Internal auditors, especially those helping in the preparation for external audit, can help and support staff to deal with the risk or accept it.

For this reason anyone working in audit, even at a junior level, needs to get as much experience as possible of the risk process. Understanding and managing risk is key to any modern organisation, so it is essential that an auditor is skilled in working with risk.

Our model IS auditor is keen to pick up on current trends and examples of risk in practice. If they have an internal audit role they try to stay in touch with developments across the organisation in order to understand the impact that changes in process can have on other areas.

Managing your personal development

If you work for an organisation of any reasonable size you probably have a manager and HR department who take care of personal development needs. You probably also have a six-month or annual meeting with your line manager to discuss your development. Most of the managers I have known have tried to be diligent in these meetings, but looking at potential needs for all their staff is very time consuming, and time tends to be one of those things that is scarce. This allows colleagues who take the time to look at what they need to continue with their own development the opportunity to indicate what their developmental needs are; not, of course, that they always get what they want – that four-day conference in Las Vegas would not justify the cost, even if they do give a presentation when they get back.

Taking control of one's development is very important. There may be requirements that differ from those of colleagues, especially in departments where the rate of change is not so fast. The audit professional needs to be aware of their knowledge gaps and be pro-active in addressing them wherever possible. They need to have an up-to-date understanding of the changes to secure business operation. This includes having the opportunity to assess various new operational solutions and processes. One of the important parts of an IS auditor's role is to be able to offer informed opinion and assistance. The ability to do that will be restricted where their knowledge is not kept up to date. Information can be gained from formal courses, but these can be costly in time and fees. However, there are plenty of professional forums online and blogs that can help to increase understanding. Some of the easiest to find are amongst the groups on LinkedIn. There are a number of professional organisations including the British Computer Society (BCS), Information Systems Audit and Control Association (ISACA) and Cloud Security Alliance (CSA). These organisations, and others, provide networking and learning opportunities as well as conferences, events and other knowledge exchange opportunities. One of the best ways to learn is from the experience and challenges that other professionals have had. Events where challenges and solutions can be discussed in a positive way can be worth their weight in text books.

It is best for a junior auditor to visit groups and others that they may be recommended to, and see which give the sort of insight that they are looking for.

Linked to this is the need to gain experience and operational understanding. This is really most important for a trainee or new person in an audit team or role. It is important that even experienced auditors do not become complacent and fall into a rut, carrying out similar audit tasks in similar situations. One way to do this is to be involved in second party audits. These are audits that an organisation carries out on their suppliers. Depending on the type of supplier, they could take a range of forms. One example might be auditing the company who provides secure disposal services. In 2008, RBS found, to their cost, that trusting a supplier to have both a sound process for secure disposal and also logs to show the chain of destruction from the time the hardware leaves the customer's premises is not sufficient.[7] Despite the fault being the supplier's, not RBS, the headline focused on the beleaguered bank. That event, and others like it, has played its part in developing the second party audit, especially for organisations who routinely deal with sensitive information.

Our model auditor is always challenging themselves. They network and look at formal qualifications, which we will look at in more detail in Chapter 4. Most importantly, they are always looking to keep up with new opinion regarding IS challenges. Nobody needs to remind them to develop their skills, they try to make sure they are aware of their weaknesses and find ways to address them.

Ability to work autonomously

Working autonomously is more than just working by oneself, it is about self-discipline to organise time and work and also critically evaluate one's own work. Some people like working under their own power, getting the support they look for from themselves. Others work best in a team where they can pool

---

[7] http://news.bbc.co.uk/1/hi/uk/7581540.stm [accessed 25 March 2015].

ideas and encourage each other. Like many of the skills, some people have personality attributes that mean they like to work autonomously; however, even these people will need to develop the associated skills such as scheduling, self-monitoring and evaluation.

When I trained as a lecturer we were taught that successful teaching came not only from delivering a class, including the preparation of appropriate material, but also from conducting a post-class review. This involved critically evaluating how that class went, which elements worked and which not, and what could be learnt overall. I kept this formal review process for most of my first year, until the pressure of work meant it got dropped. However, I always tried to evaluate my delivery to each class if only in my head during the post-class cup of tea. This helped me understand the specific needs of each class (and they were all different) as well as how effective my work was and how I could improve.

Managing your time effectively

It is a cliché to say 'time is money', but wasting time can certainly have financial cost. Where an audit is being carried out, whether internal or external, the information needs to be gathered efficiently, and the report needs to be ready before any significant changes are made that may invalidate the results. For example, if a company makes a significant change in its operations, like a change of cleaning company, while the report is being written, then any discussion that includes issues with the previous delivery of that service is mostly invalid by the time it is presented.

Another problem is, unlike in TV cop shows where each group of police officers seems to have only one case at a time, an auditor has several projects running simultaneously, all of which are important, and some of which may have similar completion dates. The auditor needs to be organised enough that they can work on several audits at once and still be effective in their work. There are also those for whom 'audit' is only one aspect of their job, so they can have many issues competing for their time simultaneously.

Timekeeping is another point of friction in a busy situation. Nobody wants to wait a quarter of an hour for the last person to arrive for the meeting to start properly. If they do arrive late, and the meeting has started, it may be necessary for the proceedings to pause while they are recapped. Where the event involves an external person the impression of the organisation can be harmed. If the manager of a data centre is waiting for the customer's auditor to come to do a second party audit of the building, and is kept waiting 15 minutes without good reason, this can harm the relationship between that manager and the customer. Where the auditor has bad self-management that can, unintentionally, appear disrespectful to those affected. This is never helpful.

Our model auditor is well organised. They try and keep a note of all the activities they are involved in and are mindful of the priorities that all aspects of their work need. They try to be on time for meetings, but let people know if they are held up. By showing respect of people's time in this way they hope to encourage others to do likewise.

Project management skills

An organisation that is being subjected to a wide ranging audit is likely to require a significant amount of work to be done over a period of time. This must be organised effectively to make best use of people's time.

While a junior or inexperienced auditor may not be involved in managing an audit project themselves, gaining experience of one is going to be essential, especially in larger organisations. The ability to manage projects, of any sort, is generally a combination of learning and practical application, i.e. a skill. There are theoretical elements that can be learnt; for example, classes on management. This may involve learning to prioritise and how to monitor and encourage the progress of a project. However, there is much that can be learnt through being involved in projects, whether as a leader or not. Setting targets that are achievable while still fulfilling the requirement of the project is key. The motivation of participants is also critical to getting the sort of rapport that allows the leader to have awareness of issues that may slow progress early, so they can be addressed. It is easy for audits, or audit preparation to get lost in the business of everyday work, a good auditor will keep the momentum going.

Our model auditor actively manages the project and them-selves, setting achievable targets and milestones that keep the project on track.

An understanding of change management

Change management is a key business skill. It is not just able managing through a change. It is about planning and recording changes and involving all relevant parties. The auditor needs to be able to look at the documentation for change management, whether procedural or technical, and be able to understand what is being done and why. They need to be able to advise if they believe there are potential issues that may arise that they have not considered in the planning phase.

I am old enough to have been at junior school when the UK currency changed from LSD, or pounds, shillings and pennies, to the decimal system. This was different from the adoption of the Euro because, unlike the pre-Euro currencies, our old system was not decimal. There were not 100 pennies to a pound. There were 12 pennies to a shilling and 20 shillings to a pound. For a while before 'Decimalisation Day' there were messages, often repeated to little tunes, on the television between programmes. Each shop had a giant currency converter board and for a while items were priced in both currencies. Also, some of the new coins, principally the 5p, which was equal to a shilling, and the 10p, which was equal to 2 shillings, copied the old coins, but with new titles. This meant that the coinage felt more familiar to people, which helped to ease anxiety. The process of preparing for this change was probably the biggest piece of change management the UK had seen. The key message was to make it trigger the least stress possible, as that would aid acceptance. Also, problems that were expected, like people having saved cash in piggy banks and big bar optics bottles, was dealt with by allowing old currency to be paid into the bank for quite a while after transition day.

Making operational changes within an organisation can be complex as one change may impact a number of areas of work. Change management is about the appropriate planning, recording and reviewing of those changes. Records of how and when major changes were carried out may well be required by a number of accreditation bodies as it demonstrates how effective the organisation's governance is in practice.

A good understanding of data analytics

An understanding of data analytics is also important as it gives a range of information to businesses that they can then use to make significant decisions. Understanding of data analytics may come easily to some, to others the learning slope may be steeper, but in all cases it needs to be understood in the context of the operation being examined. Data analytics can be used as the basic justification for change in operation, or to understand why no change is necessary. It can show the early stages of problems or strains the system may be experiencing, thus giving time for a solution to be devised and rolled out, hopefully before any impact becomes significant.

The IS auditor, especially if they are conducting an external audit, may find that the analytics form part of the narrative behind a significant piece of change management. If they are working as an internal auditor it may help to look at the cost–benefit analysis of any change, with the analysis of data forming part of the evidence to be considered.

Our model IS auditor will keep a regular check on data that shows the effective operation of their organisation. Where they see potential areas of future difficulty they will raise it with the manager concerned so that remedial action can be devised timeously.

An awareness of the spiky nature of laurels

This is an interesting comment made by one of my colleagues. If I am to be totally honest it is only tenuously a skill, but it is certainly something that is learnt and should be applied in the course of work. My colleague meant that in his experience there are times when his efforts as an internal auditor are well received. However, he said that there are other times when a very similar activity or piece of advice can cause upset and negativity between himself and operationally focused managers. Attention to detail from internal audit can lead to a co-operative and straightforward accreditation audit with all the positive feedback and satisfaction that can bring, but it may, at other times, create tension. Ultimately, it is important to keep in mind that you cannot please everyone, and the professional can only do their best and develop some ways of dealing with the bad days.

Our model auditor has had days when they are almost lauded as a hero, perhaps for identifying a problem and suggesting a straightforward solution, while on other days they are not so warmly received. They understand that, like actors, they should not get too carried away with good or bad reviews.

Maintaining a strong, current awareness of relevant impacting legislation and regulation

Bear in mind that although an organisation is based in the UK or the EU, operations can still be affected by legislation and regulation from other countries. Foremost of these are three from the USA.

Sarbanes Oxley (SoX) is a clear requirement for organisations operating from the US, but also affects organisations trading with US companies. SoX was devised in the USA to try to prevent further major accounting and fraud events after the scandals at Enron and WorldCom. It sets standards of responsibility for public corporations in the US and trading with the US. It was seen as vital that staff at board level in organisations should no longer be able to plead ignorance of significant fraudulent activities in their organisation.

The Health Insurance Portability and Accountability Act of 1996 (HIPAA) is another key piece of legislation if you are based in the USA. It is particularly concerned with the movement of sensitive data, but I came across it in my research as it was the best example of the requirement to obscure or shield computer screens if they were displaying sensitive personal data, to make sure they could not be read by an unauthorised 'shoulder surfer'. This regulation alone has had significant impact on the demand for software and hardware screen privacy solutions, especially, but not exclusively, in the US.

Another US regulation that it is important to be aware of if an organisation has dealings with a US organisation can be found in the NIST *Information Security Handbook*.[8] The auditor can be expected to ensure that the organisation has a good understanding of any legal requirements, and this is particularly important when they originate outside of the 'home' country for the organisation. Although they are not a legal authority, the auditor should have a good operational understanding of how these requirements can be adhered to in practice. Where appropriate, this can be checked with a legal specialist, but their experience is more likely to be interpretive rather than operational.

ON THE OTHER HAND

Using the idea of a model auditor has hopefully given a bit of insight into the skills and attributes someone considering

---

[8] NIST, 2006.

audit as part of their career should aim for. The skills have all come from people who work in audit now, most of whom have done so for a reasonable length of time. However, as I thought about this I realised that all of the information I have been provided with has come from inside the audit profession, and I thought it was important to get some sort of outside view also. I recently read a fascinating paper by Sarens and De Beelde,[9] which is based on information gathered from six organisations in Belgium and looks at the different perceptions on what the role of the internal auditor should be when dealing with those who interact with them, principally the audit committee, the CFO and the CEO.

Some of the most interesting skills that were suggested are worth brief consideration at the end of this section. They wanted the internal auditor to:

- Provide operational information about the organisation that was otherwise not available, especially for external directors.
- Play a pro-active role in focusing risk management on high-risk areas.
- Formulate specific suggestions for the improvement of internal controls.
- Clearly communicate about the mission and roles of IS in order to enable the creation of realistic expectations.
- Compensate the loss of control that can result from an increase in organisational complexity.
- Actively assist with the formalisation of the risk management and internal control system.
- Create a sufficient level of risk and control awareness.

What struck me about this list is that the skills are generally a good deal more pro-active than requirements I have seen elsewhere. It is worth explaining that, at the time of Sarens

---

[9] Sarens and De Beelde, 2005.

and De Beelde publishing their work, Belgium had recently imposed a new requirement that work organisations needed to have an audit committee as part of their structure.[10] The fact this was imposed may have led to some organisations wanting to utilise fully the audit function in order to make it cost effective. However, it also shows a desire for an interactive auditor who is aware of a range of organisational issues as well as regulatory requirements so that the most efficient and effective solutions are found.

We have moved a long way from that cartoon of the lone auditor with a clipboard.

An important thought

I have just laid out many of the attributes and skills that current IS auditors believe someone coming into the profession should aim for. To complete that set I think it is important to mention some skills which can be developed in the wider work environment. All sorts of experience can help, from participating in sports activities to volunteering to work with charities, perhaps in carrying out care tasks or in helping to fundraise or administer the organisation. Think back to when you were putting together your very first CV, whether for a job or a place at university. Outside interests were important partly because they added to the picture of the sort of person you were, but they also showed the sort of experiences and skills you were likely to have. An auditor needs to develop their skills and outside interests, especially if they are less demanding than everyday work. They can develop experience with, hopefully, more fun and less pressure.

INTERFACE AND DEPENDENCIES

It should be clear by now that the internal IS auditor's work depends on input from a number of other parts of the organisation. This means that, even in organisations too small to have an audit team, they need to interact to get their work done.

---

[10] Principle Five from *The Belgian Code on Corporate Governance* (2004).

Figure 2 shows that the auditor should have on-going communication with four key areas of the organisation: Executive, Operations, Support Services and Technology. As support services covers such a wide range of areas, this has been subdivided to give some idea of the sort of components that comprise that category, although these will vary depending on the organisation. In each case we will outline the nature of the relationship between the internal IS auditor and the particular area.

Figure 2 The auditor in context

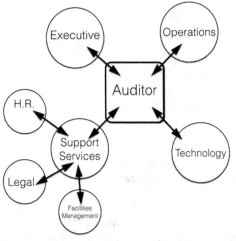

1991 was a critical year for executive governance in the UK. It was the year the Bank of Credit and Commerce International (BCCI) collapsed with a reported £5.6 billion deficit.[11] The fall-out from this catastrophic event in British banking led to a focus on the need for

---

[11] http://news.bbc.co.uk/onthisday/hi/dates/stories/july/5/
newsid_2495000/2495017. stm [accessed 19 November 2015].

increased accountability from executives. It was clear that a situation where senior staff could evade censure by claiming that they were unaware of operational details was unacceptable. If something happened within the area of responsibility for the executive then it was felt that they must be accountable. It was important that an event as significant as the collapse of BCCI needed to be fully understood, and the enquiry that ultimately led to the publication of the Cadbury Report and the Cadbury Code 1992 was instigated.

This has laid the foundation for many subsequent developments in corporate governance in the UK and further afield. The London Stock Exchange, in its guide to corporate governance,[12] identifies their own embracing of the code into their 'Listing Rules'. The guide sees the concept of a 'Comply or Explain' requirement on executives, that was at the core of the Cadbury Code, as the foundation of their approach to UK corporate governance. This means that those with executive responsibility have to take all reasonable steps to ensure that the organisation conforms to any legal or regulatory requirements that apply to them. ISO/IEC 27001:2005 reflected that same requirement of responsibility and accountability for executives.

It is perhaps a reflection of the widespread adoption of this approach that the new ISO/IEC 27001:2013 has been able to develop further and extend accountability and responsibility to the more operational levels of management. Those involved in the development of this standard describe this as more of a development to widen responsibility than replacing the executive level of responsibility with operational levels. Executives are still expected to be actively involved in ensuring the security of data within their organisation.

---

[12] London Stock Exchange, 2012.

Executive

In the light of incidents such as those mentioned in the boxed-out example of BCCI, executives of any size in organisations are no longer able to maintain ignorance of governance issues. They are accountable for such matters as the protection of information, and therefore they need to be kept informed.

One of the important roles that an internal auditor can play in an organisation is to keep the executive level informed both of current and upcoming challenges to security. This means that due consideration as to action and even the allocation of budget can be taken at a level that will make operational changes possible.

How the communication works will vary, depending on the organisation. Certainly it would be expected that a report on an internal audit would be presented to executives; probably in person in order that queries and concerns can be discussed. Some second party audits carried out by an organisation may be sufficiently important that the resulting report should be presented to executives; for example, an organisation that handles a lot of personal financial data may be particularly concerned about the disposal process, both of paper and of data-retaining technologies such as hard discs. The audit of the disposal contractor needs to be available to executives so that they can be assured that they are fulfilling their required responsibility in that area. Especially with the negative publicity given to the inadequate disposal of paper records, which began in 2008, executives have to be mindful of the harm this can do to the reputation of the organisation, as well as its legal and contractual responsibilities.

Operations

The most critical area of a business is its everyday operation. That is where data is moved, processed and thereby exposed to risk. The challenge to devise controls, policies and procedures that are going to be sufficiently operationally sound so they are actually followed by staff can be amongst the greatest in good governance.

A control that simply fulfils the requirement of an audit on paper but does not work in practice is a waste of time and can negatively affect the attitude of ordinary users to the security requirements. An ordinary, non-information-security-focused employee is less likely to look at controls and procedures and try to carry them out if their experience is that often they cannot get their job done in doing so. This means that being able to discuss possible changes with operational staff is important. Many organisations of reasonable size now have some form of 'security steering committee' that brings together representatives of those involved in the operation of IS. If there is insufficient consultation with those operational staff who are affected by a control change, problems can happen.

One health board in the UK was concerned about patient documentation being stolen or lost while district nurses were out treating patients in their homes. As a result they devised two controls: first, the nurse could only take into a patient's home those documents that related to that patient; second, the nurse could not leave any sensitive patient documentation in their car in case of theft. While both of these controls made good sense in security terms, operationally they were unworkable. The only way the nurse could follow both controls was to return to the surgery to change documents after every patient visit. Not only might that significantly affect the time required to do the work, it would be frustrating for the nurse, especially when visiting more than one patient in a sheltered scheme or home. It is the role of the auditor to identify such foreseeable flaws in controls, policies and procedures and help the relevant departments work together to find workable solutions.

In the UK the requirements of the ICO, principally as encapsulated in the Data Protection Act 1998, has had an increasing effect on operations in recent years as, at the moment, there are a rising number of publicised penalties for data breaches as businesses strive to keep up with operational challenges. One of the biggest changes in the way that staff work in the last five years has been the growth of working away from the office. In some cases, this will be when staff are travelling or commuting, but for many it takes the form of working from home. A number of elements have come together to drive this growth, including the expansion in the broadband network in the UK together with increasing speed and reliability. Also laptops and smaller devices are now more commonly used; some, as we have seen before, are owned by staff but used to connect to the corporate network for work. Unlike in the office situation, it is difficult for the organisation to control the circumstances in which people work outside the office. There may also be technical challenges from staff needing legitimate access to the corporate network from personal equipment that may not be as carefully defended against malware, or them saving documents using a personal cloud solution that they can access from work. The ICO is making efforts to make plain that senior managers and board level staff cannot divest themselves of responsibility for staff working from home. One example can be seen in an enforcement notice citing Aberdeen City Council for a breach of Section 1(1) of the Data Protection Act 1998. The situation had arisen because a member of staff was working on sensitive information on a personal computer at home. Probably unknown to the user, the information was automatically saved to a private cloud storage service.[13] This may seem like a stupid thing for the user today, but for a long time the importance of 'backing-up' data has been promoted to all users. As a result many will routinely back-up documents as a part of their work routine. Some will even have their computers set to the default of automatic back-up at set intervals. I feel that organisations with mobile workforces are going to be working hard to keep ahead of the ICO in the years ahead, and the IS auditor will need to be able to draw on experience and knowledge to help both to deal with this sort of developing risk.

The auditor needs to be aware of many operational challenges and work with appropriate staff to help them meet their requirements for the protection of data.

---

[13] The details of this case were previously set out on the ICO website http://ico.org.uk/news/latest_news/2013/council-employee-publishes-vulnerable-childrens-welfare-details-online-30082013 [accessed February 2015].

Technology

Ever since the dawn of the computerised office, IS has generally been based in the hands of those managing the technology. This is generally seen as reasonable when one considers the extent of technical risk for organisations.

The IS auditor can be valuable to the IT team by not only taking an outside view of the various access controls, user-facing vulnerabilities and management controls, but by also helping the team to consider the impact of changes in technical management and solutions on the operational concerns of other teams. While this overlaps with their operational role, as discussed in the previous section, there can be particular friction points for IT and non-IT teams. In those sorts of situations audit can help to mediate a solution.

One area that can be a particular problem can be the perspectives of the IT team and the marketing team when there is a strong online relationship with customers. The marketing team need the website to be accessible, clear and straightforward for any customer to use regardless of their technical competence. However, the IT team need any website to be resilient in its design to increase its protection against cyber attack. A good example of the potential clash in perspectives between marketing, which is outward reaching, and IT Security, which is protecting the organisation from outside attack, is how the website deals with lost passwords for accessing the customer's account. The marketing perspective wants a solution that re-connects the customer with their account as quickly as possible. This makes purchases easier, with stored delivery information, and so makes the purchase process faster and more satisfactory for the customer. It also provides valuable customer profile buying data for analysis. However, from a technical perspective, having the password reset easily through a single email communication is a weak method[14] because if an unauthorised person has gained access

---

[14] For more information on this potential weakness see Renaud and Goucher, 2012.

through a lost or stolen device then the password reminder is likely to be sent to an email address displayed on that same device. This would mean that someone getting unauthorised access to a device may not need any technical knowledge to access an online shop and order goods through the owner's account. The IS auditor will be able to look at the issue from the perspective of both sides, together with the requirements of the organisation as a whole and any compliance demands made on it, and then help to analyse potential solutions.

Sometimes the technical risk comes not from customers, but from suppliers or stakeholders to the organisation. We saw in the example of a computer disposal company working for RBS in 2008 that second and third parties can be risky on account of poor procedure in their organisations. There are also many examples of technical risks when sensitive information has

The relationship between the organisation and its stakeholders and associates can be critical to its risk exposure. Target, the giant US retailer, said that its data breach on Black Friday 2013 was caused by a third party gaining access by using credentials that they had hacked from the system of a vendor.[15] It can be difficult for a large organisation to monitor the security of their associates, but this does not mean they need not try. I am sure Target believed their security in this regard was sound, but I would also hope that it is now much tighter, while still allowing normal business to carry on. I certainly expect that other large-scale retailers, in the US and beyond, have had an intensive look at their systems to identify any weaknesses that might make them the next victim. My boss has always asserted that the very 'best' security incident for an IS team is one at the company of the CIO's golfing partner; close enough that they are well aware of the stress and the fall-out, but not bringing direct problems.

---

[15] http://nakedsecurity.sophos.com/2014/01/30/target-says-hackers-got-in-by-using-a-vendors-credentials/ [accessed 19 November 2015].

to be shared with an associate or supplier, and this has led to an increase in corporate customers requiring audits and even penetration testing of suppliers' technology before they share significant data. This means that auditors are kept busy carrying out or analysing audit reports, policies and processes. They then can provide the customer with either assurance of the soundness of the supplier, or possibly areas of concern that need to be discussed further.

There are a number of regulations and guidelines that the IS auditor needs to be able to assist the technical team with in their compliance. These include the Open Web Application Security Project (OWASP), which is most commonly used in the area of software development and application penetration testing, and PCIDSS, which has particular technical significance in relation to encryption key rotation for those taking customer payments. The Security Policy Framework (SPF), particularly at tier 4, focuses on quite detailed technical specifications, and there are also technical requirements for IEC/ISO 27001. We will look at this in more detail in Chapter 3.

Support services

Support services are those parts of an organisation that do not directly contribute to its core function. In a hospital, support staff would include maintenance, laundry and physical security staff. In a standard business organisation structure, finance, HR and maintenance departments would be recognised under this heading.

On the face of it, these services might be regarded as a weak link as far as IS is concerned. Staff are generally task orientated rather than technically focused, so in some cases can forget, or never really learn, new risks and vulnerabilities that are relevant to their operations. Although they may not deal with the day-to-day operational data, some of the information they do handle may be even more sensitive; for example, dietary requirements for a specific patient can give information about religious affiliation and the state of health of that person. This may not seem important, but if the patient is a 'public figure' such information can be much sought after by the media.

It would not be fair to give the impression that all support services are ignorant of the need to protect information, however. The protection of data has been a core part of professional training for HR staff for some considerable time. Therefore, HR professionals can often be found to be more aware of the risks and consequences of data loss than even some operational departments. IS auditors can sometimes help with suggestions about knowledge of risk and safe working behaviour to be shared within the organisation as a whole, and amongst the support staff in particular. However, not all support services can be expected to have the same perspective on the identification and protection of sensitive information as HR or finance are likely to have. Facilities management, for example, has to have particular concern for

I once inspected a facility that relied on a shared reception area with a part-time receptionist for its physical access control. In this case 'facilities management' was fulfilled by the landlord on behalf of the tenants. As far as the facilities manager was concerned, the desk was manned at peak hours when visitor traffic was highest. Outside that time visitors could be screened at the individual doors of the tenant companies. It was then the responsibility of that company to control access. However, as a result, strangers were free to roam the building looking for an open door or deliveries left in clear sight at the front desk.

This helped to keep the cost of rental of the building lower, but led to some difficulties. The ISO/IEC 27001 requirements for at least two of the tenants stated that access to the premises should be monitored and restricted during working hours and therefore a lot of discussions were necessary between all the tenants and the landlord to arrive at, and fund, a compromise solution.

health and safety legislation together with internal operational requirements including budgetary requirements. However, it may be that they have never been made aware of the importance of some of the sensitive information to which they have access. It is not surprising in that case that staff do not always take great care with what they may see as unimportant information. In that sort of situation, it is surely the fault of the employer for not communicating effectively, rather than the staff member for not acting in accordance with guidelines they are not aware of.

It has long been known by social engineers that support services, such as external maintenance companies and cleaning and catering agencies, provide some of the easiest modes of access, both physical and virtual. It is therefore essential that the IS auditor is able to engage those working in facilities management in the secure working process.

When we look at all of the areas that the IS auditor needs to work with, the size of the potential challenge becomes apparent. Even when all parties are keen to work together to protect data, their, sometimes conflicting, operational requirements can make finding workable solutions difficult. While it is not the role of the auditor to make those decisions, their guidance and support should be a valuable resource to the organisation as a whole.

3 TOOLS, METHODS AND TECHNIQUES

So far much of what I have discussed has been with regard to the IS auditor as an individual, what skills and attributes they need to bring to the role and what is expected of them if they are to be successful. Experience, analysis and judgement are important to all of these. However, for the auditor there is additional 'weaponry' to help in their defence against insecurity.

Yes, it is true that the 'weapons' are tools, methods and techniques of achieving secure operation, but they can be powerful if used with knowledge and skill.

If I had just said that the auditor could choose from a variety of standards and frameworks that are in common use in larger enterprises, that does not sound very powerful or interesting does it? However, not only should an auditor be prepared to work with a range of standards that are required by external bodies such as customers and potential customers, they should also use some of the elements of these standards in devising effective internal audits.

I have listed below a number of frameworks and standards and provided brief descriptions as to the areas where they apply or the uses to which they can be put. If any are unfamiliar, and yet sound interesting or helpful, then clearly looking at the standards and frameworks in full is recommended. These points are just stepping off points – it is up to you to make the journey.

STANDARDS

There are a range of standards that the IS auditor may need to audit against. The main ones are:

- ISO/IEC 27001:2005 and ISO/IEC 27001:2013;
- ISO 22301 – Business Continuity;
- ISO 17025 – Laboratory Standards;
- TIA942 – Standards for Data Centres;
- SSAE 16 and ISAE 3402 – US standards for controls that are used widely for security;
- HM Government Security Policy Framework (SPF);
- UK Public Services Network (PSN).

ISO/IEC 27001:2013

This is an international standard that addresses information security management. It aims to promote good management of secure data handling as a dynamic process within organisations. The standard encourages an organisation to be constantly looking forward strategically, in order to plan regular reviews and improvements of their processes. It was devised to relate to all aspects of operation of an organisation, not just those parts that may appear to have a higher risk of exposure to data loss. Indeed, it could be argued that the holistic approach of this standard is one of the reasons for the growth of the 'culture of security' within business. ISO/IEC 27001 is not evaluated in terms of a 'how to' checklist, rather it is about presenting, and providing evidence of, operationally effective controls.

When it first appeared in 2005, the notes of introduction described the desired approach as being a strategic plan for 'preventive action'. In the updated 2013 version this wording was replaced with 'actions to address risks and opportunities'.[1] This implies that the controls and processes to be devised should not be seen as a one-off action, like the building of a defensive castle wall. Rather, by addressing risks and opportunities, which are themselves dynamic operational concepts that need regular monitoring and reviewing, it signals a change of focus away from a standard that is achieved, a certificate issued and then mostly forgotten about until the next review. The new standard encourages the achievement and maintenance of this standard as an on-going process, evolving as risks change.

As with SPF, ISO 27000:2013 can be used as a standard or as a framework. ISO 27000 is a standard, ISO 27001 contains the requirements that an organisation would be audited against in a compliance audit. ISO27002 are a series of recommendations for best practice, but are not compulsory. Many organisations that are not currently taking the accreditation route may still choose to use the standard as a framework.

ISO 27002:2013 is designed to give:

> Guidelines for organizational information security standards and information security management practices including the selection, implementation and management of controls taking into consideration the organization's information security risk environment(s).[2]

What is the point of certification under ISO/IEC 27001?

The first and often the main reason is that a customer, or a potential customer, requires the assurance regarding the care of data that this standard is designed to give. Another reason can be that key people within an organisation feel that they are at the stage when it would be beneficial to formalise their IS processes in a way that will be recognised externally. This latter can start slowly with the review of current practices to bring them into line with ISO 27001, and move on to establishing

---

[1] www.bsigroup.co.uk/en-GB/iso-27001-information-security/ISOIEC-27001-Revision/ [accessed 19 November 2015].

[2] www.iso.org/iso/catalogue_detail?csnumber=54533 [accessed 19 November 2015].

new policies, procedures and controls that will further secure operations. One benefit of this approach is that it can be kinder to budgets because any required investment can be spread over a longer period as there is no externally set deadline for accreditation such as might come from stakeholder pressure.

Where to start

The first action that needs to be taken, whatever the motivation for the project or the timeline involved, is to identify the risks to IS that the operation of the business, technical and non-technical, expose.

At this point bring together someone who is familiar with the standard, someone who has a good understanding of the business processes within the organisation and an appropriate technical specialist. They can form a core base from which to reach out to other areas and specialisms within the business and assist them to come into line with the requirements for secure practice. An internal auditor will bring knowledge of the standard and should also have knowledge of the internal processes and therefore can help to bring these aspects together. However, if the organisation is of any significant size, they are likely to need specialist assistance – at least while the process gets going. It is also essential that there is management 'buy-in' across the organisation and up to senior, including board, level. They need to be able to provide support and, where necessary, investment to ensure that the preparations for the certification process result in more secure operation in the future.

Collaboration and co-operation

These have to start very early and need to stay the course of preparation and implementation. Certification under ISO/ IEC 27001:2013 has expanded its requirement for accepted responsibility to senior managers as a development from executive level management (who were drawn into the process in ISO 27001:2005). The rationale behind this cascading of responsibility is that, in order to be most effective, the standard must be supported at the highest operational levels as well as at strategic decision-making levels, i.e. it has to be a key part of how the organisation operates.

For some organisations, the challenge of finally bringing the responsibility for the security of information out of the IT domain and sharing it is not a huge one. Perhaps the nature of their business, for example in a healthcare organisation, means that all staff have some awareness of the need for care and discretion. However, in established organisations, sharing of the responsibility for data security more widely can be quite hard to do successfully.

The challenge of 'keeping it going'

One of the hardest challenges for an internal auditor is to encourage and maintain momentum for improvement after the external audit has taken place. Sometimes compliance audits can be viewed like an exam, with the exam day being when the external auditor makes their visit. Most people forget a great deal of what they learn for an exam straight after it, if there is no need to remember. If audited staff think in those terms it can be difficult to maintain the commitment. ISO/IEC 27001:2013, along with other standards of the ISO series, looks for evidence of on-going compliance such as incident logs and post-incident reviews demonstrating how the organisation deals with new or unforeseen challenges, so it is vital that staff continue to operate the processes and controls.

One consideration in maintaining the overall commitment is when time commitment is reasonable. Where there are meetings that need to be regular, but not necessarily frequent, then this should be reflected in the meeting schedule. Where meetings continue to be held frequently long after anything is achieved, then support from attendees, who have other demands on their time, will be reduced. For example, there is a requirement for routine meetings to review the incident logs. These meetings are important as it is critical to learn lessons, such as defence against and recovery from incidents. If they are efficiently run and properly recorded they can prove to be a valuable tool for the improvement of operational processes. If they are badly run and attendees feel it was a waste of time, support will fade.

It is helpful to recognise that ISO/IEC 27001 can be used to form a framework without the need to take the accreditation step at that point. Taking the decision to use the framework first can help the organisation, its managers and its executives to understand the risks and the operations. This ensures that processes can be designed around potential future accreditation, or indeed provide information that a customer may need for their current accreditation.

ISO 22301

This standard addresses business continuity planning. Business continuity is about resilience, not defences. It looks at how the business plans deal with a disruptive event when it happens, not about preventing the event happening. Modern businesses cannot hang up a metaphorical 'closed' sign until the problem can be dealt with or mitigated. Business must go on, and business continuity plans aim to make disruption as small as possible.

What is the point of certification under ISO 22301?

Making such plans is also about being able to demonstrate to stakeholders, including present and prospective customers, that the operations of the organisation have resilience. This means that plans are in place to prevent significant incidents leading to long disruptions to operation; and this means that the service they expect will be delivered as quickly as possible even if there is an unforeseen, disruptive incident. Some tender requests will require this, and indeed it is not unreasonable to do so from the customer's point of view, considering that they want to be assured delivery will continue with minimum disruption. Companies offering off-site, or cloud storage of back-up data are expected to have contingency plans to deal with physical disruption at the site, such as a fire, as well as technical disruption, such as damage to data cabling into the site. A customer needs to know how quickly they can expect operations to resume after a significant event, and will often choose the provider with continuity planning as a key factor.

When business continuity first became an area for business concern, many organisations focused on the impact of a technical loss, either of data or of connection to it, and questions such as how long they could continue to operate and at what level. This was sensible as technology was a lot less stable and having a key network server fail, disrupting most, if not all, work, was much more common. Now, various events, such as weather and major infrastructure failures, are routinely included in such plans. As I write this, some parts of the south of England have recently experienced the wettest start to a year for a very long time.[3] Looking at pictures of the floods and listening to stories of the logistical and other problems this has caused makes me think that business continuity has become more 'real' for many in the last few years. For many organisations, business continuity is becoming more than a good idea. It is an essential part of planning.

The winter of 2010/11 saw unusually heavy snowfall in areas of the UK that were not used to it. Also, once on the ground, consistent low temperatures meant that ice and snow compacted and made road and rail travel difficult for a long time. This affected a lot of organisations, who found their staff took so long travelling to and from work that the amount of work that could be done was much reduced. However, some organisations had already improved their continuity planning after the swine flu epidemic the previous year, which resulted in many unable to come into work, arrangements were made so many were able to work from home. The investment in laptops and virtual private network (VPN) connections that happened as a result of the issues caused by this event meant that business journeys could be reduced in bad weather with less impact on the operation of business.

Where to start

Just like ISO/IEC 27001, the starting point for this standard is to identify those risks that might reasonably interfere with the ability to operate at optimum efficiency. These may be risks that the organisation has some control over, such as the delivery clauses of any contractors or suppliers used. Another

---

[3] www.metoffice.gov.uk/climate/uk/interesting/dec2010.

significant area to be checked is data storage and back-up. For example, if this is carried out by a third party how often is the process for restoration from back-up exercised? What is the guaranteed time to restoration and what is the supplier's plan to implement their BCP? Some organisations can be surprised to find that they may not be the priority to their off-site data storage contractors. As they may not be able to change this, they need to make their own plans to cover possible downtimes.

With business continuity it is important that an organisation understands the expectations of its stakeholders and customers because these may be different from those driven internally. For example, in the event that the main office for an organisation is damaged by fire, the external stakeholders may be interested in the operation of the business returning to normal as soon as possible. The organisation itself may agree, and be able to find alternative office space quite quickly. However, as soon as requirement for elements such as canteen provision and meeting spaces are added, the selection may prove harder and therefore longer. In other circumstances the organisation may believe that their customers expect that, in the event of a major incident, they will return to delivering at the normal rate very quickly; whereas their customers may actually be willing to tolerate a slight delay to their delivery time as long as normal delivery is restored once the problem is dealt with. This is a slight, but possibly significant, difference between actual and anticipated expectation, and that difference could result in significant extra, unnecessary cost. This means that communication becomes a key element in the BCP.

Collaboration and co-operation

As with ISO 27001, this standard cannot be devised, operated and maintained by a small group within the organisation. Everyone has to be involved.

To begin with, it is necessary to gather information from all areas of the business regarding what they would find to be a disruptive event. Then mitigating and restoring actions need to be devised and discussed with those who would need to carry them out. If the plan involves people working from home, it is important to know if any key workers live in an area with slow connectivity speeds, or even cell black spots.

Once the plan is devised it needs to be practised and all those who might be involved need to be trained so that precious time is not wasted through mistakes and misunderstandings. To take a practical example, if you get on any commercial airline you will have a safety briefing. Although all that the passengers really need to do is to respond to the direction of the highly trained crew in the event of an emergency, it is still believed that all passengers have to be instructed in advance. Once the emergency happens, it is a bit late to start working out how to fasten your life jacket or blow your whistle.

The challenge of keeping it going

Once certified to the standard it would be easy to sit back and neglect it. After all, the measures outlined are only required when there is an interruption to delivery. However, things change all the time, which means that a BCP needs to be reviewed at regular intervals. For example, if the organisation had a BCP devised in 2011 that included provision for remote working if the office became unavailable due to some form of significant damage, was the use of mobile devices incorporated into that? Were there considerations included about what information could be accessed remotely and if this would be affected by whether the device was owned by the staff member or the organisation? Is the same set of circumstances relevant now? Such issues need to be addressed before the alarm goes off.

It is also important that senior management have a good understanding of the BCP and help in its upkeep; for example, by encouraging staff to keep their contact details up to date. One of the best ways of keeping the plans fresh and relevant is to run occasional exercises involving key personnel. This does not need to involve closing off buildings and thereby affecting normal operations (although this can be useful if there is a slower time of year when it would be least disruptive to run), it can be a table-top exercise. If well planned and run, these exercises can focus staff attention on the BCP and any challenges to its effectiveness, which will allow it to be revised where necessary.

ISO 17025

This is a standard that is specifically designed for testing and calibrating laboratories. An auditor is likely to come across this standard in relation to a supplying contractor such as a computer forensics laboratory. An aspect that is singular to this standard, at least amongst those examined here, is that it evaluates the quality of the practices carried out in the laboratory. It asks questions such as:

- Are operations carried out in a consistent way?

- Is the recording of events consistent with the requirements of the process being undertaken? This is important to be able to track faults and errors.

- Are the instruments or tools calibrated accurately so the results are meaningful outside of that situation?

If we take the example of a digital forensics lab, we can show the role of this standard. Within that lab there will be an on-going requirement for clean, new hard discs to be used for imaging 'suspect' discs so that copies of suspect hard discs can be analysed in a legally sound way. Most shop-bought 'blank' discs actually contain some data. This is not significant for general use, but where a hard disc is being copied for examination then it is vital that the hard disc the information is copied on to is entirely clean, and therefore the perfect copy. Although discs will be bought and brought into the laboratory in sealed wrapping, it is still possible that, for example, there is test data or even pre-existing data from earlier customer use that failed and was returned to the vendor. Of course, it is essential that all discs are checked before use. In practice, the best way to do that is for all new discs to be routinely cleaned before being suitably stored, ready for use. The procedure for doing this needs to be clear, operationally sound and consistently applied by trained staff.

Technical requirements, such as those for the cleaning of new hard discs, form one of the two sections of this standard. On the whole, these requirements are specific to the laboratory being audited and will include baseline competencies in technical operations for all staff working in the laboratory. This ensures everyone is trained and that training is regularly refreshed in a way that is appropriate to individual roles.

It is also possible, depending on the work being carried out in the laboratory, that there will be a requirement for proficiency testing between compliance evaluations by their accreditation body. This means that staff must demonstrate their skills in certain key activities together with their on-going personal development in the area in which they are operating. A straightforward check that might be helpful for a 'visiting auditor' from a customer organisation, who may have limited knowledge of the process happening in the lab, is to see that all the processes being carried out are covered by the terms of the existing accreditation and that the laboratory has not operated outside of the work they were certified to carry out.

The second part of this standard focuses on management requirements. This is vital because the technical system might be entirely compliant, but if the way that tasks are carried out is not appropriately managed then the standard of the actual operation is at risk of inadequacy. This part relates to the ISO 17025 'operation and effectiveness of the operation management system'[4] and will be along similar lines to any quality management system. It asks questions such as:

- How is the overall quality of work monitored and reviewed?

- What is the mechanism for any necessary improvement or other changes to be approved by the accreditation or professional body?

---

[4] http://www.iso.org/iso/home/store/catalogue_tc/catalogue_detail.htm?csnumber=39883 [accessed 19 November 2015].

This, even without in-depth technical knowledge, will give some insight into the reliability of the work of the laboratory.

TIAIS942

This is a standard for data centres. Although it originates from the USA it is generally accepted as the standard for all data centres. It covers:

- site space layout;
- cabling infrastructure;
- tiered reliability;
- environmental considerations.

An auditor may need to be aware of this standard either because their organisation operates, or is planning to operate, a data centre themselves, or because they need to be assured as to the quality of the data centre they are sub-contracting.

The information from this standard may also feed into the BCP for the customer organisation as it specifies the accessibility of the centre as well as its own continuity of supply and fault tolerance. Indeed, the requirement for future demands to be considered in the provisioning of the centre means that the customer can be more assured of long-term availability as demands for storage for all types of customer increases.

SSAE 16 and ISAE 3402

These standards are very similar and it is advised that an organisation have one or the other. They give information on policies, procedures and controls to customers and potential customers. In some cases this information may be required by the customer to fulfil their own certification requirements regarding their suppliers. For example, information about relevant policies and procedures from a sub-contractor handling the disposal of their confidential waste will inform part of ISO/IEC 27001:2013 documentation for the customer.

The bodies behind these two standards, The American Institute of Certified Public Accountants (AICPA) and the International Audit and Assurance Standards Board (IAASB), have been working to draw the developments of these standards together to a point where they are aligned. At the current time, Deloitte describes SSAE 16 as mirroring ISAE 3402.[5] As this growing alignment is internationally recognised it is very unlikely that any organisation would be required to provide evidence of conforming to both.

Maturing is a very important point in these standards, and for a customer audit by someone less familiar with the standard it is a point to be aware of. They have been designed so that organisations having a newly designed or implemented system can provide documentation specifying its controls and procedures even though the system has not run long enough to provide information on the effectiveness of these controls and procedures. Once the system has 'matured', meaning it has been operating for more than six months, then the information generated can provide evidence for a more thorough assessment. These two levels of standard are called Type 1 and Type 2.

Type 1 is the first stage, the stage before there is evidence of the effectiveness of the system in operation. It is simply a description of the policies and procedures of an organisation and the design of its associated controls. These controls will vary, depending on the nature of the business and its operations, but will probably include financial controls and demonstration of good governance.

As the purpose of the controls has to be specified by the organisation itself, it gives more freedom for them to fit with their own operational needs. However, it must be realised that information put into the application for this stage is essentially theoretical, with no requirement of practical demonstrations. In some cases, the system may have been operating for up to

[5] ISAE 3402 and SSAE 16 (Replacing SAS 70): Reinforcing confidence through demonstration of effective controls (2014). http://www2.deloitte.com/lu/en/pages/risk/solutions/isae-3402-ssae-16-examinations.html [accessed 19 November 2015].

six months, but that would still be regarded as 'settling in' and not provide sound evidence of how the system will operate routinely. Type 1 certification is of limited, but important, use. It encourages organisations to create sound systems from the start, and gives them benefit for that.

Type 2 is the 'Mature' stage of these certifications as it reports on the operation of controls that have been running for more than 6 months but less than 12 months. The reason for the limit on the running time is because the external audit will be required every 12 months to ensure it most accurately reflects the current operation of the organisation.

This requirement for regular evidence of operations means that achieving certification of this type is much more demanding on the organisation than some certifications as it involves significant input from across the organisation. The external auditor will require written assertions or statements from appropriate managers regarding the operation of controls. These will then need to be verified with logs and other documents so that the auditor can satisfy themself that the control is being operated as specified. These statements or assertions are the key to this certification. They are the link between the controls and procedures and their day-to-day practice.

The requirement for the maintenance of routine evidence gathering, such as the keeping of good records of incident management meetings and incident logs, can have additional benefits to the organisation. Any customer requiring a second party audit can be assured that the system is monitored and records are up to date. That will make their task easier; indeed, it may not be necessary for them to conduct a full audit themselves when the evidence of regular certification to these standards can be provided. They may only need to examine the audited documents to ensure they provide the information they require.

Security Policy Framework (SPF)

The SPF comprises a standard, guidelines and general approaches that are required to be applied to government departments and agencies and those who answer directly to them. It also can be extended to public bodies such as local authorities and emergency services. It is included here, rather than in the section on frameworks, because it can be used by any organisation, whether they intend to work for government or not. However, for those who are working within, or for, government it is mandatory and so is best viewed as a standard.

Until the most recent SPF release in April 2014 there were a number of mandatory requirements. An internal auditor has the opportunity to play a vital part in trying to find ways of meeting these requirements in an operationally effective way. Of course an external auditor will also have that knowledge, but does not have the same internal knowledge. The mandatory requirements meant that the framework was quite rigid, which – while making the checking of compliance reasonably straightforward – made it difficult for some organisations to be able to demonstrate compliance, in particular given the diverse nature of organisations to which the SPF applies. The most recent version of SPF, however, takes a different approach. While the required outcomes are mandated, the means of achieving them is not. This does provide much more flexibility, but still expects that the standard operation is high and the operation of the organisation is sound.

If we look at each of the mandatory outcomes in turn we can identify some of the challenges that they may present to an internal auditor or audit team.

- **Good governance** – Good governance describes a situation where those with oversight of areas of particular concern to key stakeholders are not only aware of those significant internal and external issues that affect their area of responsibility, but are actively monitoring any appropriate changes that may be required.

  Good governance is dynamic; it can be likened to the way a good pilot maintains control, or governance, of their aeroplane. At times they may be just monitoring systems while the autopilot controls navigation, but they are ready to react to any situation that requires their input to maintain the safety, stability and integrity of the plane. Likewise, an executive with responsibility for human resources will need to monitor advice from the ICO regarding the handling of personal data and ensure that any required adjustments to organisational process are implemented to ensure the safety and integrity of personal information.

The importance of governance oversight of data security has been seen as critical for some time now. The fact that governance has now been cascaded to middle level management, as specified in IEC/ISO 27001:2013, has important implications for data handling. For some organisations the identification of 'information asset owners', as required by the SPF, can be difficult to implement, especially if the data is stored externally. The fact that actually having information asset owners is mandated gives a clear statement about the need for good governance of the security of data at all points in the data process. This includes, for example, the oversight of destruction of hardware.

The requirement for a senior manager to be responsible for providing good governance can help to achieve a higher priority for solutions in budget and process design.

• **Culture and awareness** – While a significant part of the protection that is provided for data in a modern organisation comes from technical design of system-secure technical processes, a lot depends on the way staff carry out their work and how aware they are of the potential threats to the security of sensitive data.

This human element was seen as so significant in the operation of the financial sector in the UK that the Financial Services Authority required that all staff of organisations registered with them demonstrate that they have significant awareness of security threats and good secure practice. Oversight of this area has now transferred to the Financial Conduct Authority. A culture of good security, often abbreviated to a 'culture of security', is a work environment where good awareness is a key part of how work is done with all staff having a protective attitude to information.

This is then re-enforced by example and peer pressure amongst staff. This is especially apparent with new staff who learn the culture from those around them; that is, by watching what they do and how they behave. Peer pressure just means that those who do not work in the same way as everyone else are encouraged to do so. The idea of encouraging a culture of security is that getting secure practice as the normal way of working helps to achieve a situation where good secure practice is part of the 'way we do things here' attitude. Both these user-focused elements in assuring the security of information come from all staff playing their part by identifying and managing risk and accepting personal responsibility for protecting against those risks.

Security culture and awareness is not necessarily easy to test as results of the absence of incidents can be difficult to record. An experienced auditor will be able to evaluate probable effectiveness of the security awareness programme that is being used and make observations of the general behaviour of staff; for example in activating screen savers and hiding passwords.

An auditor, especially an internal auditor, can use their experience and knowledge of the framework to help managers to identify areas of particular operational risk and consider the options for raising awareness; bearing in mind the need to be able to demonstrate good culture and awareness in a way that meets the standard's requirements.

• **Risk management** – It may seem obvious to say, but risk to the IS of an organisation needs to be identified, evaluated and managed if managing processes and controls are to be effective. It is this area where experience of both operational practice and the framework are essential. It is therefore a situation where a 'new' auditor needs to gain as much experience as possible. The fact that the new SPF allows organisations to set goals, rather than prescribe ways to achieve them, means they are able to find solutions that best fit effective business operations. However, there is a greater emphasis on being able to demonstrate how the controls, policies and procedures work to meet required outcomes. This is much more difficult than just meeting mandatory requirements as due consideration of existing business operations is required. The importance of risk management is that it is managing a risk, not just identifying it or accepting it; it is dealing with it in an appropriate way.

- **Security of information** – This outcome references training as well as the appropriate classification of information. While some staff, such as those working in HR or finance, might be aware of the sensitive nature of some of the information they handle, many other staff may not be. This can mean that some staff might not recognise the information they are handling as the sort of material that needs careful handling. Even a guest list for a dinner may contain contact details and dietary requirements, the latter of which might indicate health or religious and cultural information that is protected under Schedule 3 of the Data Protection Act 1998.

It is an important part of the role of the auditor to evaluate whether the guidance, training and processes are helping to achieve the ultimate aim. They can offer advice as to the effectiveness in the planning and implementation of the organisation's training. However, it is vital that the design fulfils the requirement that staff be able to identify sensitive information that they may handle in the course of their work. If they are not able to do that then it is much less likely that they will be effectively working to protect that data.

- **Technology and services** – While not all technology and technology services in an organisation will use the internet, its existence means that the security of technology architecture and solutions needs to be more rigorous to protect information from potential outside attack through any internet facing access points.

The existence of criminals who focus their efforts on using the internet as their method of gaining access to data or money or both means that it is essential that all organisations who handle sensitive information, especially 'citizen data', are particularly careful with the design and implementation of their technology. Implementation is an on-going process and, for the purposes of SPF, should be subject to an annual review, so it is vital that security updates are processed in a timely and effective manner. The auditor needs to ensure that these are appropriately logged and reviewed.

- **Personnel security** – Some organisations that are subject to the SPF framework have staff who handle data sufficiently sensitive that it is necessary for them to be put through an appropriate level of HMG security clearance. Organisations that require this will have a process to acquire clearances for staff, or validate claimed clearances from existing staff.

  Where formal clearance is not required there should also be processes in place to ensure that staff handling other sensitive data have all their references taken up and relevant claims to qualifications checked. Although this is not fool proof, it can help to weed out the most obviously untrustworthy applicants. Sometimes the need for quick recruitment can make this difficult, but having a robust process of regular review of personnel records to ensure that CVs are properly checked before any probation period is complete can help to limit the risk. Also, the maintenance of access controls, which restrict access to certain documents or document groups to make sure that only those who currently need access have access, can contain any potential unauthorised viewing or copying of documents.

- **Physical security** – When thinking about the assurance of data security the physical protection of the environment in which it is stored or used can be somewhat overlooked in comparison with technical security. However, good physical security is essential. After all, if an unauthorised person can remove a computer or a storage disc they do not have to worry about hacking in through firewalls or other protection.

Routine physical security measures can be amongst the hardest to review internally. When one gains access on a regular basis it takes a practiced eye to spot any vulnerable elements. It is often the case that someone wearing a uniform that identifies them as a courier or a specialist maintenance person can get access to a building with significantly less identity checking than other visitors, for example[6] An auditor needs to be aware of these weak points and work with the responsible departments to strengthen security in a way that endeavours to restrict the operational needs of staff as little as possible.

- **Preparing for, and responding to, incidents** – It is important for any organisation to have controls and procedures in place to deal with incidents; however, these are only effective if they are rehearsed or practised. The most common example is fire drills. These must be run routinely in public buildings to make sure that all regular users are aware of how to react safely in the event of an incident. This level of preparation can make a significant difference to the number and type of injuries sustained in the event of a real fire.

In the same way, preparation for security incidents has to be carefully planned and practised. Staff should be aware of how to identify a potential incident and how to make a report. Some of the most difficult incident issues can be where the incident results in restriction of access, whether that is physical access to a building or technical access to a system.

Where the cause of the incident is less obvious than a fire (for example, resulting from a criminal action

---

[6] Long, 2006.

that requires the area to be restricted while it is investigated) restriction can be met with resistance by those who have their own tasks to carry out or have left personal belongings that they want to retrieve. Having rehearsals for key personnel, whether in real time or in a table-top workshop exercise, can make it easier to deal with that sort of issue.

These exercises can also be useful for virtual threats, such a malware infestation that has a significant impact on the working of the network. It may be necessary for the network to be shut down for a while as the problem is dealt with. It can be particularly useful for staff from areas that would be significantly affected by the knock-on effects, such as the finance department, to be involved so that they can make their own plans as to how to handle such situations. For example, a call centre may not be directly affected by a cyber attack on the organisation's system, but it may mean that the information accessible to staff becomes significantly restricted. Running a practice exercise will allow the call centre management to consider the best response to different levels of impact in advance. These options are then fully thought through and ready should the need arise. This makes it possible to react more quickly, which may be essential, particularly when dealing with a cyber threat, and to minimise the disruption to normal operations that may have been one of the aims of the attack.

Ensuring that the internally generated solutions to these mandatory outcomes are fit for purpose requires the knowledge and experience of a range of people and the IS auditor has a key role to play in that. It is their position of being slightly outside 'looking in' at the processes that can be so useful in evaluating the effectiveness of proposed solutions.

Public Services Network (PSN)

Any organisation that deals with central or regional government has to demonstrate compliance with the requirements of the

PSN. The PSN is a programme run by the UK government that ultimately aims to create a network infrastructure that will enable organisations who deal with central and regional government to share access to core information and services.

The government has good reason for being very careful about the protection of data. Where sensitive data is being shared across a single network, as in this case, the impact of a significant incident could be widespread. The publicity that a significant incident would gain is enough in itself to concentrate minds on including the strongest possible governance of the PSN. As a result, the requirements for accreditation to the PSN are not a development or an extension of any existing commercial certification; they are stronger and more prescriptive.

Someone approaching the task of bringing an organisation into line with the requirements of the standard will find many of the requirements difficult to de-code without help. It is, of course, possible to read books on the subject, but the information I have from people who work with the standard is that the most efficient way to learn how to approach it for the first time is to go on an approved training course. This will give you the opportunity not only to get the information you need, but also to get answers to questions and think through important issues that commonly arise.

I make no apology for suggesting that someone faced with a standard they are unfamiliar with takes steps to get formal training in it. It can often be more cost effective to do this rather than 'picking it up as you go along', which can slow down work and lead to mistakes. Think carefully about the training you use; get recommendations for companies if possible and consider the approaches that best suit you. Some people learn well from computer-based training (CBT) and tuning into web-based discussions and tutorials, while others need to be in a more social setting in order to become more involved in the subject.

Payment Card Industry Data Security Standard (PCIDSS)

The PCIDSS is a crucial standard for any organisation holding payment card data. It covers all areas of the payment 'environment' including people, processes and technologies involved in the storage or processing of this sensitive data. It requires an annual review and, as processes and technologies of organisations change, it is important that the auditor keeps in touch with any changes to the standard or to the organisation that may affect their compliance with the standard. For example, as the PCI Security Standards Council says, 'The use of a Payment Application Data Security Standard (PA-DSS) compliant application does not itself make an entity PCI DSS compliant'[7] – organisations must still meet a range of very prescriptive requirements.

The important thing for an auditor to be aware of is that this is different from most other standards in that there is no operational flexibility. So, while SPF has mandatory outcomes and the method of achieving those must be operationally effective in the context of the organisation, PCI DSS really is a 'tick box' exercise in compliance monitoring.

This can be a good area to allow junior team members to gain some experience as less experience and judgement are required. However, more experienced advice may be required in preparation as the inflexibility may result in operational compatibility issues. These can come about where an organisation believes it must work in a way that means it does not comply with the requirements of the standard. Experienced advice will be required to guide the organisation to meet the requirements.

---

[7] PCI Security Standards Council, 2013.

BEST PRACTICE FRAMEWORKS, PROCEDURES AND PROCESSES

Focusing effort on some areas of an organisation that are more exposed to the risk of data loss may lead to neglect in budget and in security practice in others. This can be magnified when the focus is on achieving accreditation or certification. Fortunately there are frameworks that support effective operations in all parts and functions of an organisation. The difference between standards and frameworks are that a standard is something that has to be achieved itself, while frameworks enable organisations with complex operations to bring order, identify weakness and develop further in a strong, safe way – especially where there is a strong interplay between technology, systems, operations and interfaces with other organisations who have their own complex systems. If frameworks are properly implemented, maintained and monitored they can help businesses function in a more efficient and effective way, but each one is only as good as the implementation. It is the role of the IS auditor to understand these frameworks and guide and advise the organisation to an effective implementation.

It follows, therefore, that an IS auditor needs to have an understanding of the main frameworks in case they need to assist an organisation in implementing one. It is worth noting that a single organisation may have to design their operations around a number of frameworks because of the requirements of their key customers. Also, there is the possibility of a need to conduct second party audits to confirm secure practice from their suppliers. A supplier may be using a framework that is different from the one the customer uses. While this is not generally important, the auditor carrying out the audit of secure practice will find it easier if they understand the framework the supplier is using. They will know where to look for key information and the sort of processes they should expect. In the last year there have been new versions of ISO/IEC 27001 and COBIT 5 and the latest edition of HMG's SPF.[8] I suspect, with the continuing rapidity of technical developments

---

[8] Cabinet Office, 2014.

and their effect on business and security, the amendments and changes will continue to appear.

The IS auditor also needs some awareness of non-security based frameworks, such as those based around Six Sigma, Total Quality Assurance, ITIL, 'Best Practice', Management by Objective or any other trendy 'management fad' that is passing through town that year, as these will affect the 'home organisation' audits and second or third party audits.

Some frameworks are imposed because of external factors, such as the need for those working with UK government to comply with the requirements of SPF. However, others are tools that can be used by an organisation to implement a structure that will help to produce evidence more easily that will be appropriate for current or future compliance needs.

While it is possible to devise a bespoke framework for an organisation, it is often better to use an existing one that can be adapted to the individual needs of the organisation. The IS auditor should have some understanding of the most common frameworks so they can help advise their organisation as to efficient ways of adapting to using the framework.

Below are three examples of frameworks. In each case I briefly outline the framework, how it works and what it seeks to achieve. In both cases greater detail is best gained from the source websites, which are referenced.

COBIT 5

COBIT 5 focuses on the management and governance of an organisation as well as balancing risks and benefits. As mentioned above, sound governance and the engagement of management can pay big dividends in terms of taking a more corporate approach to any operational issue and this is particularly important with security issues. It means that risks are identified and action can be taken to identify the best way to approach those risks, including possibly accepting them, but always in the context of the operational requirement of the organisation.

Consistent with many of the standards cited earlier, COBIT 5 incorporates IS and security into all aspects of the business enterprise operation. There are specific guidelines for the security and IS aspect of the framework, but these apply in the context of a holistic approach to organisational governance.

COBIT 5 is based around five core principles, as shown in Figure 3, and all other aspects of the framework are developed from these. The COBIT 5 framework works by being based on core principals and guidance as to how a framework can be built around them. There is a model framework, but it is a guidance tool. An organisation needs to design their own framework based around the guidance from COBIT 5, but which still allows the organisation to operate effectively.

Figure 3 COBIT 5 principles[9]

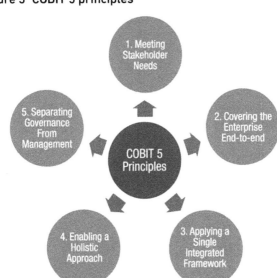

Source: COBIT 5 ©2012 ISACA. All rights reserved. Used by permission.

---

[9] www.isaca.org/Education/Online-Learning/Pages/A-COBIT-5-Overview.aspx

The key principle is that the framework that is devised must meet the requirements of relevant stakeholders and the organisation's operational needs. If these requirements are understood then the framework should improve secure practice while still allowing the organisation to function optimally. This is best achieved by understanding risk and by including the governance of that risk in the core operation. That means that the risk is managed on a day-to-day basis.

For the framework to be most effective, a good understanding of why it is being devised in the first place is important.

For example:

- Is it to enable the organisation to demonstrate compliance with a particular standard?

- Is it to give greater protection after a data breach?

- Is it simply that the time has come for IT governance to be managed in a more systematic way?

An internal IS auditor will be able to help the organisation to identify possible issues that can arise with some controls, policies and procedures in their situation, and thereby can save time and effort and not a little frustration. If some requirements are overlooked then these may not be designed into the basic framework and will have to be added later, which is generally less ideal. An example might be the possible outsourcing of data storage, which, in the early stages of the framework design, is still under discussion but has not yet happened. If it is felt very likely that this change will happen, and the current discussion is really about details such as which provider to use, then including it in the framework of governance is a smart move.

There is a large suite of elements to COBIT 5 including COBIT 5 for Risk and COBIT 5 for Implementation. The part that is relevant here is COBIT 5 for Information Security. An auditor working in any aspect of COBIT 5 can not only study the relevant documents, but also access podcasts and discussion forums to get a feel for how this framework is used in a range of situations – beneficial when time allows.

Open Web Application Security Project (OWASP)

This is an open source project that focuses on improving the security of software, not only traditional software programming, but also software application programming for mobile devices. The drive behind this is to promote an understanding of the importance of incorporating security at the design stage of software development rather than trying to bring security features to existing software.

Some of the guidance from OWASP is, quite reasonably, very technical, but the core principles can be incorporated into frameworks to promote security. It is included in this section on frameworks because it provides a potential appendix to an existing framework for those organisations that develop software as part of their core operation. An IS auditor should be familiar with the general principles of OWASP because they may find that they are, or are planned to be, incorporated into the frameworks that they audit, whether internal or external.

OWASP's 'Green Book'[10] has a number of requirements that have been built in to address those elements of governance that specifically apply to government bodies, including the following:

- 'The Government Body <u>must</u> establish and enforce a standard that requires application security for organisations and applications under their jurisdiction.

- The Government Body <u>must</u> build application security into software acquisition guidelines.

- The Government Body <u>must</u> provide OWASP a "notice and comment" period when releasing laws and regulations that are relevant to application security.

_____
[10] OWASP Foundation, 2013.

- The Government Body <u>must</u> define or adopt a definition of application security.

- The Government Body <u>must</u> create and promote public service messages focused on application security.'

Its recommendations are:

- 'The Government Body <u>should</u> be an OWASP supporter.

- The Government Body <u>should</u> assign a liaison to OWASP.

- The Government Body <u>should</u> encourage educational institutions to focus on software security.

- The Government Body <u>should</u> leverage OWASP by attending events, using materials, and asking experts for help.'

While these are not universally accepted recommendations, the growing requirement for security in all types of software development, including apps, means that it can be reasonably expected that some of these requirements may be reflected in standards in the future. An IS auditor with knowledge of this specialist sub-framework may be able to advise their organisation of elements that may be relevant to the development of their own processes.

Information Technology Infrastructure Library (ITIL)

This is an established framework that aims to bring together IT services and management systems to make business operation more effective, not least due to a more robust IT system that works with the operational requirements. ITIL focuses its guidance on five 'lifecycle phases':

- **Service strategy** – This involves solid planning, incorporating both operational needs and IT delivery capabilities, to maximise the business benefit. Key to this approach is to understand the organisation *and* the market it serves, or is seeking to serve. Market demands may, for example, drive the need for particular IT capabilities such as mobile customer access. Strategic planning is about understanding forthcoming requirements and positioning the organisation to meet these effectively. An auditor can help in implementing ITIL in a number of ways, including the provision of an organisational overview and knowledge of other external compliance standards that the organisation, or their customers, may need to meet and that may impact on their operation.

• **Service design** – As you would expect in a process-driven approach, this is the phase where the strategic requirements are designed into process. It is essential that the requirements are fully understood and incorporated. It is not uncommon to find that those requirements that are perhaps not headline, but still crucial are forgotten, leading to organisations incurring significant cost later in the design process.

The auditor can play an essential role at this point by analysing the system design and the strategy to ensure all aspects are considered. There may, for example, be a requirement for the design to use approved elements, such as a firewall prescribed by the customer, and that may not be one with which the designers are familiar. These sorts of prescribed requirements become increasingly problematic to include after the initial design, as was mentioned in relation to COBIT 5. For example, a service transition is going to be planned based on the initial design for the new framework. If a criteria is required by an external stakeholder and is not identified at this early stage it might be difficult to include later.

• **Service transition** – Where new services are to be brought into the system the means of testing, adjusting and implementing these can be very challenging. Indeed it may involve not only technical design and change, but the training of non-technical staff and the provision of new user guides.

It may even be necessary, if there is a critical user interface, to plan an increase in 'customer help desk' staff for a transitional period. For example, where a bank enforces the introduction of a token authentication device for users accessing their account from their computer, customers may be confused and need reassurance and guidance for the first few times they use the new devices, even with the provision of a user guide and possibly a 'how to use it' video on the bank website. The auditor can use their experience and knowledge to help to highlight those issues and their likely business impact.

- **Service operation** – This is the delivery of day-to-day services. It is important that operational issues arising are logged and reviewed at appropriate intervals so they can be addressed either in present operation or considered in future design developments. It may be that external accreditations have specific requirements as to the content and process of incident logging and the auditor is best placed to ensure that these requirements are fully met.

- **Continual service improvement** – It is important that the provision of any service should constantly aim to improve. However, this can be challenging. In terms of design, how much can the existing provision improve before fundamental changes and possibly a redesign of the system are required. Any improvements will come at a cost and the knowledge of the IS auditor can be critical in ensuring that any changes that are planned to improve the service delivery will meet any existing or expected compliance requirements; thus keeping overall costs as low as possible.

In all these phases the communication skills of the IS auditor, as well as their position of being external to the actual design and implementation activity, allow them to make a valuable contribution to the efficiency and effectiveness of the operational processes of the organisation.

4 CAREER PROGRESSION AND RELATED ROLES

As I said at the beginning of this book, some people take a deliberate decision to become an IS auditor and some find that they acquire the role as part of their job description and move across gradually. Those finding themselves moving into the audit role are most likely to have a managerial role within the IT section. This is generally still regarded, in many organisations, as mostly the concern of technical folks. As we have seen, the protection of data is everyone's problem in the modern organisation, but breaking the 'magnetic field' that draws all things IS back to IT is a long campaign that you will pull and push against.

ENTRY

There are two main stepping off points for a career in audit.

Internal

You may have joined an organisation as part of an audit team because audit is a deliberate career selection for you. You may be fresh out of education, or changing the path of your career so far. In this situation you should expect to focus on assisting with internal audits or preparing the organisation for external audits.

If the organisation is not a large one, or one focused on the need to be certificated or accredited, you may have audit as only part of your role. Most likely you would work in IT, but it is possible, not least because of the increasing demands for data protection from the ICO, that you work in the HR department. Having audit as part of your role in the beginning can be ideal as it gives you a taster of what the role involves and allows you to decide if it is one you would want to focus on primarily in the future.

External

The audit function in some organisations is much more outward-facing. An example of that sort of company is a consultancy that gives assistance to other organisations. The audit team is likely to be guiding their customers through a range of audit situations. Joining this type of organisation is a bigger decision to make in terms of career choice as you are going to be working in an audit team most of the time, whereas in other organisations audit may form only part of your role.

On the other hand, this situation is more likely to put you into a team of auditors from whom you can learn and gain experience. You can start at a junior level and develop your audit skills through an established career development plan. As organisations sell themselves on the quality of the staff they can provide to customers, it is in their interest to focus on the development of their staff – the more qualified they are, the better rates they will attract. It may, therefore, be easier for you to access training courses and external events that will add to your experience and knowledge.

CONTINUED PROFESSIONAL DEVELOPMENT

As has been mentioned in a number of contexts already, the IS auditor needs to ensure that they continue to improve their knowledge and skills in order to offer the best advice and assistance.

Not all of this knowledge will come from formal professional courses. For someone working in an internal audit role, taking the opportunity to get insight into areas of their organisation with which they had little previous experience may be as valuable as a day spent in a 'classroom'. It can be enlightening to talk to staff who have customer-facing roles and hear their experience of IS in their day-to-day work. There are times when those endeavouring to give the highest standard of customer care find conflicts with IS policy; for example, do they feel pressure to talk to someone who claims to represent the customer, but has no formal authority to act in that place? Understanding that sort of situation can help with the design of better training and support of staff, even where the rules protecting access cannot be changed.

There are a range of other situations where the auditor may gain insight and understanding outside the pursuance of professional certification. These include attendance at professional networking events and events where information on skills, standards and frameworks will be discussed. Some of these will be reasonably local to the auditor, while others may be based at a population hub such as London. In each case, the value of the event and the cost of attendance can be assessed against probable gains in knowledge. There are also a wide range of regular web-based seminars and discussion groups that are more flexibly accessible to the individual. Some examples of sites that are worth keeping an eye on are ISACA, ISSA, Microsoft, Bright Talk (who do some very good online presentations), any information security vendor (including Alien Vault, McAfee, Cisco, Symantec), and there are plenty of others; it really is a matter of looking around and finding the site or company who is raising issues of concern to you or maybe who provides information in a form that you like. They might be a vendor your organisation uses, but the choice is quite individual so have a look at the smörgåsbord and take your pick.

However, as with any profession, it is a good idea to gain the core knowledge of the practice and approach to the role by following a professional certification. There are two main professional certifications, IRCA and CISA. Both of these certifications put a strong emphasis on the need for continuing personal development.

International Register of Certified Auditors (IRCA)

IRCA is a division of the Chartered Quality Institute and its certifications are designed to demonstrate a professional's qualification and competence to carry out their role. All auditors within the scheme, in whatever area of specialisation, need, on each review, to demonstrate proficiency in five areas:

- educational qualifications;
- work experience;
- audits;
- training;
- CPD.

This is based on a mix of study, on-going development and competence through experience. To get certified, you need to apply to IRCA and include evidence of training as well as work experience. You also have to submit a personal statement demonstrating your knowledge of, in this case, IS auditing (the application form is generic for a number of sectors requiring an auditor role). Current issues, requirements and influences in the sector should be included to show that you understand the IS sector.

In the IRCA scheme for IS audit there are three basic levels of auditor:

- Provisional Auditor;
- Auditor;
- Lead Auditor.

These are different depending on whether the candidate is an internal or external auditor. However, there is no hierarchical difference between being an internal auditor or an auditor who principally conducts external audits and there are parallel paths for these two environments. Progression to the highest level is by a combination of training and involvement in audits. This can be represented in a diagram as in Figure 4.

Figure 4 Career progression for an IS auditor

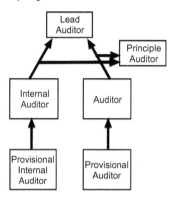

The Provisional level indicates that the candidate has attended appropriate training courses, but has yet to conduct any formal audits. This level, therefore, is for the inexperienced new arrivals to the profession. It is not expected that anyone would stay at this level for an appreciable length of time as they will soon become involved in audit activity.

Someone at the Auditor level, whether internal or involved in external work, is expected to have conducted a full systems audit if they are a general IS auditor, or audited part of their organisation's system if they are an internal auditor. It is expected that an internal candidate at this level in most organisations will have the audit role as a significant component of their job or as their full-time task. While it is important for auditors at this level to gain experience of leading teams, it is not expected that candidates have responsibility for the audit work of others without assistance or supervision.

The Lead Auditor level requires the practitioner to have further qualification and experience in the role and also to lead audit teams or manage an audit process.

Then there is the role of the Principle Auditor. This role has slightly changed in its definition recently and is there to recognise experienced auditors who do not lead audit teams. They may conduct significant audits in terms of scale or importance, but do that on their own rather than as part of a team. It also recognises those who may have been active auditors, but have now progressed to working in other areas of audit such as the design of audit systems. Those conducting officially recognised and quality controlled IRCA audit training are also recognised at this level.

It is important for IRCA to have this level because it means that those who have a lot of knowledge and experience in the audit area are still recognised and are encouraged to maintain their knowledge at a current level. However, it is a sort of sub-level rather than being in the chain of development as most with an IRCA certification will be active auditors or lead auditors and have no wish to take a step away from the operational role.

As you might expect, given the variety of information required for an application, the process has a significant administrative element and it would benefit provisional candidates to be guided by an established auditor in the first instance to ensure that they submit the right information in the appropriate way to make their application effective.

Certified Information Systems Auditor (CISA)[1]

This is a certification that comes from the ISACA (formally known as the Information Systems Audit and Control Association) suite of certifications. The approach of CISA is very different from that of the IRCA in that it has at its core an examination. A CISA candidate needs to pass the exam and have five years of appropriate audit experience;[2] however, it is common for the exam to be taken before the five-year mark.

---

[1] www.isaca.org/Certification/CISA-Certified-Information-Systems-Auditor/Pages/ default.aspx

[2] There are exceptions that can reduce this time in some circumstances, including those with recognised academic experience or education. Refer to the ISACA website for up-to-date details.

Once CISA is gained, it has to be maintained through continuing professional development. ISACA encourages their members to consider gaining their other certifications, such as Certified in Risk and Information Systems Control (CRISC) and Certified Information Security Manager (CISM). The idea of an audit professional being encouraged to expand their knowledge, not only to a wide area of the organisation, but also in sufficient depth to pass an internationally recognised examination, will increase the credibility and, to be perfectly honest, the commercial value of the candidate.

The popularity of this certification, both with applicants and with recruiters, has quadrupled in the last decade. The certification is one of the suite of qualifications administered by ISACA. The importance of CISA in the business world today includes:

- Giving formal recognition of the knowledge and experience of the holder.
- Indication that the holder has a high level of expertise in the audit area.
- Confirmation that the holder takes effort to ensure that their knowledge is current.
- CISA as an internationally recognised mark of professionalism.

In many places in the course of this book I have talked about the advice an auditor can give, the assistance they can offer and the insight they can bring to critical decisions regarding the security of data in the business world today. Following the high-profile data leaks that first gained prominence in 2008, and continue to provide column inches today, the security of data has become something that an organisation does not as a courtesy to its customers, but as a way of protecting the reputation and the legal position of the organisation. When stakes are that high then auditors need to be not only highly professional and competent, but also able to prove that.

'MODEL-BUILDING' GUIDANCE IN THE REAL WORLD

The days when career progression meant a school leaver joining a company and 'working their way up', increasing their income as they progressed, are largely over. We are all part of a more mobile workforce now. It is expected that staff will move between companies during their career, sometimes as a way to promote their career. This means that it is important that people can track their career progress, and check for development suggestions using some external, yet widely accepted, tools.

One of the best tools for someone wanting to develop IS audit as their career is the Skills Framework for the Information Age (SFIA); a framework for personal development that can be used either by the individual or the organisation to guide the development of a candidate across a range of skills and experience. As was suggested in the section on building a model IS auditor in Chapter 2, a good auditor needs to be constantly looking to increase their knowledge and understanding of standards, frameworks and changes in the risk environment for business. The information SFIA contains provides insight into new skills to be developed and experience the auditor should be looking to acquire. It can help a candidate to identify gaps or areas for development in their skill set, helping them to grow their career.

SFIA is designed to be understood by general managers and HR specialists as well as those IT professionals who would expect to benefit from it more directly. It is not only a framework for IS audit, but also covers a wide range of work for a candidate in IT-associated positions. As has already been noted, the internal auditor may have audit as only one aspect of their job portfolio; SFIA allows them to map other aspects too and plan development activity that may give benefit to more than one facet of their job.

There are six basic skill categories:

* strategy and architecture;
* business change;

- solution development and implementation;
- service management;
- procurement and management support;
- client interface.

SFIA looks at a full range of IT and professional development and so covers much more than is needed in guiding an auditor. In this schema, IT audit encompasses IS audit and comes under the heading Procurement and Management Support. There are seven skill levels. These levels are numbered and labelled using general terms:

1. Follow;
2. Assist;
3. Apply;
4. Enable;
5. Ensure, Advise;
6. Initiate, Influence;
7. Set strategy, Inspire, Mobilise.

The basic information for each level is described under the headings:

- Autonomy;
- Influence;
- Complexity;
- Business Skills.

The precise definition for each of these at different levels will vary. For example, if we look at level 1 – Follow, Autonomy, it is defined as 'Works under supervision. Uses little discretion. Is expected to seek guidance in unexpected situations'. A candidate at this level would, clearly, be a total novice who has little knowledge or experience to guide their action.

Audit requires a range of pre-existing knowledge and experience across an organisation, as we have already discussed, and so it should not be a surprise that someone wishing to move to this skill area should be able to operate at level 4 – Enable. So, a new candidate should be expected to have the following proficiencies:

- **Autonomy** – The auditor has autonomy of operation, but is entirely responsible and accountable for their actions. They have clear objectives set for their work but the decision of the approach to meeting those objectives is one that they have personal control over.

- **Influence** – The auditor has the knowledge and experience, as well as the communication skills, to have influence both internally with colleagues and specialists from other teams and externally with suppliers and customers. They may have some responsibility for the work of others, although they are probably only leading a project within a team, rather than leading a team. Nevertheless their decisions in this role can be critical to the success of projects and the successful functioning of the team in that situation.

- **Complexity** – It is expected that the auditor is involved in a number of complex activities in a range of situations. They will be able to identify and analyse the issues involved and provide, or guide others to provide, a solution that fulfils required objectives.

- **Business Skills** – The auditor must have developed the level of skill in business operations that allows them to carry out their role successfully. As was identified when we devised the 'model auditor' earlier in this book, communication skills and an understanding of the business processes relevant to the role they are undertaking are vital. They must also have a good understanding of any standards they are generally required to use and a basic understanding of others that are applicable to areas of business they may have dealings with. These could include supply firms on which they might need to carry out second party audits. An understanding of, for example, ISAE 3402 and SSAE 16 would enable a second party audit to be shortened, as much of the evidence that is likely to be required will be available as evidence for their current accreditation.

These SFIA levels are there to enable development, so there must be aspirational targets. These include, under level 5, that the auditor be capable of more autonomous work using their knowledge and initiative of building business relationships and understanding the relationship between audit and the wider organisational requirements. This is where we can really see the start of the IS auditor as a net contributor to the effective operation of an organisation. They also have responsibility not only to maintain and develop their own skills, but those of their subordinates as well.

For the purpose of modelling I have been looking at the role of the IS auditor as an isolated one, as if someone in this role would be entirely focused on carrying out that function. However, as we have discussed, for many this may not be the case as in many organisations there is no requirement or, perhaps more realistically, no budget for a dedicated audit role. This means that most 'auditors' will be able to map their current job to a number of different roles on the SFIA scale. For example, someone working as a manager in an IT area may be operating at level 5 in the IT management part of 'Service Strategy', but when the audit role becomes part of their job specification they may require the sort of supervision and support more aligned with level 3, at least for a while. This combination of roles across the SFIA framework can make exact mapping a challenge, but one that may in fact be even more important for all that. When the level 5 IT manager first has to add some audit responsibility to their role it can sometimes be difficult for them to justify the support and collaboration which they are convinced they require, but which their headline role indicates is probably unnecessary. Giving the practitioner a method of demonstrating where their skills need to be developed or re-enforced can help justify courses or conferences that could be valuable in that development process.

PRACTICAL EXAMPLES FROM SFIA

At the moment the SFIA framework does not identify the role of IS audit explicitly, but we can look at the suggested requirements for technical audit, which requires essentially the same skills, and extrapolate from there to see how an auditor might develop.

Level 4 is the entry level for technical audit and that means that the skills required are those set out in the previous section. At this stage, the auditor is probably educated to degree level and has about two years of relevant experience, perhaps in IT or business process. They will take part in a range of audit activities, including audit planning and the risk process, and will broaden their knowledge with training, especially of aspects of business operations and processes with which they are less familiar.

The key point at this level is the requirement to acquire both knowledge and experience of the general operation of business, i.e. how the different elements interact and interdepend. The auditor also needs to understand the importance of stakeholders and how they can influence the approach to operation of a business and the impact that external factors, such as technical and legal changes, can have on an organisation.

By the time the auditor has moved up to SFIA level 5, the skills and attributes they demonstrated at level 4 will have developed, and they will be gaining proficiency in higher level skills, such as evaluating risks across the business and being able to contribute to the organisation with their advice and assistance in dealing with those risks.

A good understanding of the risks of a business is fundamental to helping an organisation evaluate whether it is sufficient to understand and accept the risk, put controls in place to meet those risks or have processes in place to mitigate the impact of the risks. Of course, it may be necessary to both defend and prepare mitigation, but that will depend on the risk and the organisation's operational needs.

At level 5 the auditor must be capable of producing reports of sufficient accuracy and quality that they can be presented to any interested parties, including at executive level. An auditor looking to be recognised at level 5 will be able to identify and evaluate complex issues and analyse the effectiveness of the solutions in terms of operational need and accreditation or other audit requirements.

As the auditor moves between levels 4 and 5 they should pay particular attention to the development of their professional audit training, examples of which are discussed in Chapter 3. The important thing at this stage is that they gain industry-recognised training and certification for their professional knowledge and understanding while getting as much experience as possible of making a positive contribution to an audit process.

By the time an auditor has reached SFIA level 7 they are planning and managing significant audit projects and they have the respect and experience to be making a positive contribution to the operation of an organisation. Some may have the opportunity to influence outside agencies and organisations through their membership of professional bodies and the respect in which their professional colleagues hold them. The recent revision of ISO/IEC 27001 was carried out with the assistance of professional auditors with plenty of industry experience and knowledge of business practices.

An IS auditor at level 7 will be expected to be proficient in problem solving at both tactical and strategic levels. This is particularly important if they need to work at executive levels where strategic planning is important. The executive level connection can generally be taken, in larger organisations at least, to be a sign of the consistently high standard of the work of the auditor as well as the value the board places on their insight, their oversight and their reliability overall.

This auditor will also be expected to help in the development of less experienced auditors in their team. They would be expected to review audit documentation from work carried out by others and offer assistance and guidance where appropriate. Someone achieving this top level will be educated to the post-graduate level of Master. The precise area of study is less important than the demonstration of analytical and communication skills that this level of qualification requires.

Although an auditor who is recognised at level 7 has achieved the highest point in the framework, they are still expected to maintain a strong understanding of those risks and operations that are relevant to the environments in which they perform their tasks. They should also ensure that they are aware of issues that may prove challenging to the business in the future. Businesses are generally planning several years ahead in strategic terms. If there are issues approaching that may have an effect on those plans it is helpful if they can be considered.

An example of future potential risk is the growth of 'Smart Building' technology; that is, the growing ability to control the operation of a building through technology. This can potentially lead to significant efficiencies in the operation of buildings, but there are also security considerations, especially where the controls for the building can be accessed remotely. This presents the possibility that the system may be hacked and damage to operations caused. These issues are only now beginning to be addressed,[3] but those moving into new buildings with this sort of technology need to ensure they understand both the risks and the benefits.

As previously mentioned, all auditors should, to the best of their ability, attempt to keep their knowledge and experience up to date. This will make them most relevant and helpful to the organisations with which they work.

---

[3] Lee, 2014.

5 CASE STUDY 'A DAY IN THE LIFE OF AN AUDITOR'

Just as in any other job, an auditor can spend days on the phone, in meetings and trying to get through emails they really should have dealt with at least a week ago. While this is realistic in many cases, it does not really reveal a lot about the role of auditor. What I have devised below is an entirely fictional account of a day in the life of three auditors: Jo, a junior, relatively new member of an audit team; Mike, a senior auditor; and Sam, a lead auditor. In this case the auditors all work in the same internal audit team, but, as will be explained, some of the events are very similar to those experienced by an external auditor. Pulled together in this fictional account, their experience makes a day that we may consider a very tough day – I certainly hope that not every day is quite this eventful.

Jo has been a member of the audit team for just six months, having come straight out of university with a BSc in Business Information Technology. He is currently committed to audit as a career in the medium term but, if pushed he admits that his ambition is to achieve executive level in a significant organisation using both his business and technical knowledge and skills. Having settled into the team he is keen to gain the experience to go forward for professional certifications as soon as possible.

Mike is one of the senior auditors on the team. He has a BA in Management and an MBA, and he also has a good depth of understanding of technical, business and operational security. He has a lot of experience in business and has worked in a number of organisations including a public sector organisation. Mike finds that his depth of experience and management perspective can be a useful contrast to some of the more technically focused members of the team who sometimes struggle to put the technology in a business context. When working with other parts of the organisation on internal audits it can be very helpful that he can present himself as a non-technical person. Generally, Mike likes to arrive a little ahead of time and sit in the canteen having a cup of coffee and checking his personal emails and any blogs and publications that inform his work as he finds that he does not get time to concentrate on them once he gets to his desk. Mike often works with Jo, who shadows him taking notes in meetings and on audits. He also checks and discusses Jo's work with him when he has gathered information himself to input into an audit. This can sometimes be frustrating to do, but Jo is a fast learner so on the whole mistakes do not re-occur that often.

Sam is an internal lead auditor in this large organisation and has had audit as part of her role in the IT team for about eight years. Sam loves the challenge of strategic planning. She has grown to enjoy this part of her role more and more as time has gone on. She would say that it is her area of strength and having the opportunity to lead large-scale projects, both IT projects and those involving her using her audit skills, is both the biggest stress and the most fulfilling part of her current role. Like Mike, she also takes the opportunity to get in ahead of most of the crowd to check her emails and websites of interest and organise her day before the phone starts to ring.

Our day is one of those Tuesdays that follow a bank holiday, which means that it has the regular meetings that are scheduled on Tuesdays because it is generally a calmer day than Monday, but also those issues that would appear on Monday. There is the added problem of people being on holiday. All in all there is the potential for this to be a busy and frustrating day.

The day starts with the weekly audit team meeting, which was moved from Monday. It is the time when tasks are assigned, on-going projects discussed and reports reviewed. These projects include a second party audit, an access control review, a review of outstanding 'gaps' identified in internal audits, investigating a new supplier who claims ISO 27001 compliance (and has internal audit reports available) but has not undergone (and currently has no intention of doing) certification audit and the routine review of the security incident system.

It is a particularly important time for Jo as issues are discussed including work he has been involved in. It gives him the opportunity to benefit from the experience of the others and to understand the organisational or operational issues that need to be considered in finding solutions. On this occasion, however, phones keep ringing with team members being required so all that is really achieved is the assignment of tasks. (I realise that in theory people might turn off their phones, but realistically – and I checked this with a number of people – in this sort of situation the most that is generally expected is that the sound is turned off.)

Jo is pleased to be a late substitute in a second party audit in the afternoon as one of his colleagues is off ill. However, this means that there is only half a day to get other things done that have built up. The main task is to produce a paper for Sam explaining which certification would be his preference to start with, what he believes is involved and explain why he thinks this is the appropriate place to start his IS audit studies. Jo had expected to be told what the learning process is in the team, but colleagues say this is Sam's way of making sure that new staff understand what they will be doing and the time and effort they will need to commit. Jo also sees it as a way to show his analytical skill and commitment.

After the team meeting, Mike just has the chance to make an important phone call to an external supplier to confirm the audit visit for the afternoon, and then is straight into a meeting with the manager and key staff from the sales team and the IT team. The purpose of the meeting is to discuss a recent preliminary audit that highlighted the amount of data being accessed off-site by the sales team and to understand the nature of the data being accessed as well as the risks and benefits. The meeting turns into quite a dynamic discussion about the support and security education that sales staff need and the best way to ensure that this is provided in an efficient and effective way. Although staff have company mobile devices, so technical controls can be implemented, it turns out that procedures regarding internet access using public WiFi and the process for reporting lost devices is not well understood or followed by sales staff. Some devices have also been found to have Dropbox or other cloud storage apps installed. These appear to be favoured by staff over the 'approved cloud'.

It is important that technical personnel get some understanding of why staff seem reluctant to use the approved cloud, especially if these include technical reasons such as usability issues. It may be necessary to include the training team in future discussions to see if training can be made more attractive to, and effective for, sales staff. This sort of meeting can be tricky because the IT team and sales teams have conflicting motivations. While the sales staff are generally incentivised by financial reward for volume of sales, which means they are unhappy with anything that affects this such as the restriction of access to data while mobile working, IT, on the other hand, has responsibility for the technical protection of data, which generally means they prefer to restrict its movement, especially outside of the organisation's premises. As a senior auditor, it is Mike's job to try and take an objective view of the discussion.

While this meeting is going on, Sam is trying to get on top of her emails, many from senior managers and requiring a phone call follow-up. Sam finds this sort of catch-up time both vital and frustrating. Of course, the shortened week affects everyone in the organisation, not just the audit team. However, the nature of audit queries, being generally non-critical, means that on a busy day they are likely to get a lower priority than Sam really needs. With the pattern of the four-day working week, everyone is busy and it can be really hard to get hold of all those she needs to speak to. One of the people she is very keen to catch is Andy, the senior operational IT manager who is currently in the meeting with Mike. Sam arranged with Mike to catch Andy before he has a chance to get lost in his own personal in-tray.

At the end of the meeting Mike asks Andy to drop into Sam's office for a quick cup of coffee. Sam has identified a potential issue in the change management log. The entry was in relation to one of the IT team who had been given specific authorisation to make a critical system change during working hours; a potentially risky operation. However, the log indicated this work had been carried out while the authorised person was at a meeting with her at a contractor's premises. Sam did not want to formally raise this issue immediately as there could be a simple reason for the apparent discrepancy; indeed, the log could have just been incorrectly completed. To make sure she has a clear understanding of the situation Sam feels it is much better to have a quick, informal fact-finding chat at this early stage.

This is a potentially serious issue as accurate logs are vital for many reasons, almost least amongst them being the requirements of accreditation. Also Sam is aware that the audit team needs to promote the idea that they can make a positive contribution to the business and therefore needs to try to limit any image of auditors as being some form of organisational policy enforcer. Luckily, Sam and Andy have worked together on projects over the last few years and there is a good degree of mutual respect. Andy also appreciates being given the opportunity to manage the problem in his team. He promises to deal with the issue and meet again later in the week.

Emerging from the meeting with Andy, Sam has a couple of voicemail messages to respond to and then has to be back at her desk to review more documentation. As lead auditor, a lot of the documentation resulting from internal and second or third party audits needs to be checked to make sure that it has been correctly interpreted and to see if there are wider implications that may need to be addressed. This is especially important as the information will not only be used for the internal audit, but may also be called on for reference by senior managers. As the team leader, it is part of Sam's role to feed back any significant observations she has on the reports to the documents' authors in order that they continue to improve their skills. For example, they may have made reference to an identified issue, but not made it clear why this issue is significant in the context of the audit.

Meanwhile, Mike makes another attempt to contact the data storage contractor to confirm the meeting for that afternoon. However, the person answering the phone does not have access to the appropriate diary to check that arrangement and has gone to try and contact the right person. There is the promise of a return call, but clearly if that does not come soon then the meeting may have to be re-scheduled. Mike gets the impression that there might be some significant issue happening at the data centre that is making it difficult for him to contact any of the senior managers. He is understandably curious as to what that might be, and makes a mental note to try and find out if this was the case when he visits. This might give him insight into how incidents are handled, which is useful to the review. However, he will have to wait and hope to get a return call soon. He lets Jo know that grabbing a sandwich early might be a good idea in case they have to eat in the car because of a re-scheduled meeting. This visit has already been cancelled once so Mike is keen to be as flexible as possible to avoid cancellation again

By the time Jo is back with the lunches the call has come through from the data storage centre and, as Mike expected, the meeting has been brought forward to 2 pm, so they need to set off quickly. Jo has not quite finished his paper for Sam about courses, but hopes that he can have a good discussion with Mike on the journey as he has plenty of certifications himself. However, as a late substitution to this inspection review, Jo has to be filled in as to how he is expected to behave and record their findings, and Mike uses the time in the car to do that.

This is not a full inspection; there are some issues that arose in an earlier inspection, principally regarding inadequate locks used for the cages containing the storage discs and the wiring to those cages being unprotected and therefore vulnerable to interference. At the time of the inspection, remedial actions for these issues were agreed and this visit is to check on the implementation of those actions. If they are not in place it is possible that an alternative data storage provider will be considered in the future, which would not only be bad for the provider, but would also lead to additional work for IT and audit teams in advance of the change. For both sides it would be better if this inspection went well. However, Mike has to make sure his inspection is thorough as any incidents that arise as a result of something he misses will be something he has to answer for. So, all in all, this is a high-pressure visit.

Sam grabs a lunch in the canteen then manages to get back to one of the people who had left voicemail messages in the morning. It is an external customer who needs some information for their ISO 27002 audit. This results in quite a long and detailed phone call and then Sam has to send a follow-up email with the information that has been agreed.

When she gets back to the department she finds there is discussion about an on-going audit review of another supplier. One of the new practitioner level members of the team is having her first experience of being involved in such a review and appears to be unsure of her ability in the matter. Although Sam is only involved in part of the discussion she realises that this is a matter she should concern herself with. She then has a private discussion with the new team member and offers one of the senior team members to support her in order to ensure the quality of the work she undertakes and to provide feedback.

Sam has another meeting with one of the senior staff from HR and another member of the IT team. The issue under discussion is the development of a new 'Mobile Working Good Practice Guide'. This is really something that IT and HR need to agree on themselves; Sam's role is to ensure that they are mindful of policy and of legal and regulatory issues. At this point the critical discussion is about the development of guidance that will be acceptable and followed by those using their own devices as well as those using devices owned by the organisation. This guidance will be less effective if it relies on prescriptive rules, as transgression cannot reliably be detected, especially on BYOD devices; however, there are legal and regulatory requirements to make all reasonable efforts to protect sensitive data. This is a difficult meeting as any solution is likely to leave someone at the table less satisfied than they would like to be. Sam also has a solid end-time as she has to be available from 4 pm to talk to Mike and Jo when they get back.

Mike and Jo are pleasantly surprised that, after the last-minute timing issues, the site inspection is very well organised. The person who accompanies them is well aware of the critical issues and is able to discuss the process they went through in order to implement the agreed solution. Mike and Jo are allowed to see the cages and assure themselves that the solution has been applied to all storage that is relevant to their organisation. There is a noticeable release of tension from all sides at the end of the visit.

During the journey back Mike discusses with Jo what they have seen and how that should be recorded. They agree that Jo will draft the necessary documentation and get it to Mike as soon as possible so it can be finalised and on Sam's desk the next day.

Mike and Jo manage to get back just after 4:45 pm and come straight to Sam's office to feed back on the visit. Because of the critical impact on secure operations that would result from the data centre not dealing with the issues satisfactorily, Sam has promised to inform the CISO the same day of the preliminary result of the inspection. This would enable any necessary decisions to be taken at board level regarding the on-going relationship with that supplier very quickly if the storage remained unsatisfactory. Sam lets the CISO know the position, and assures him that the report on the visit will be ready for the executive meeting at 2 pm the following day. This, of course, means that Jo and Mike will be busy through the evening and first thing tomorrow to ensure that the report is of the appropriate standard to be distributed at that level. Mike knows Jo has a lot of ambition and is said to be quite smart, and this is a situation when he really hopes that is true. If the draft document from Jo is not up to standard there will not be a lot of time to explain gently how he can improve it in future while still encouraging Jo for the effort he has made.

Before she leaves, Sam likes to double-check that desks are cleared of unwanted sensitive documents because she sees the implementation of this straightforward process as indicative of the underlying security attitude of the team. If someone in the team is pushing documents out of sight, for example in an unlocked drawer rather than in a locked cabinet, then she needs to keep an eye on that behaviour. If they are simply acting without due care, they may just need a reminder of procedure and the reasons behind that. However, where a staff member has previously been meticulous in their actions, such that this sort of oversight is uncharacteristic, this might indicate they are discontented or possibly suffering from stress and they need some additional support. It is a simple observation, and not fool proof, but it can help a manager deal with issues early and discretely before they affect the team or have a more serious impact on the individual's health.

Sam grabs her coat and bag and runs for the door, only to meet her boss in the lift. They stand in the reception area having a 'bit of a catch-up' for 15 minutes. Sam finally gets away and runs to the station hoping that the general delay in the train departures at the end of the day means that she can still catch hers. No, it left on time and she has to wait for the next one. Well at least with her smartphone she can catch up on emails.

AND SO...

That is an IS auditor. Whatever level they are operating at they need an eye for detail and a determination to balance good governance with operational reality and work with, rather than dictate to, the organisation as a whole. The role is a challenging one, but it is one that can add much to the effective and secure operation of an organisation.

The challenges of security and information assurance in the modern enterprise are huge and are growing not shrinking. The days when a company just needed a good strong lock on the filing cabinet are long gone and with this increased risk there is the need for someone to guide the defence. Someone has to check that the walls of the castle are not flaking or that someone has not built a hut on the outside of the wall because the view is better.

You may not consider auditors to be the most popular people in your organisation; they seem to make a lot of demands on people who are probably working as hard as they can anyway. But all that seeming interference and pedantry, if done by a well-qualified and experienced professional, may ultimately save everyone a great deal of grief.

I will finish with my favourite memory of IS auditors: at an ISACA conference in London in 2013 with an international vice president bringing the house down with his performance at Karaoke and the rest of us raising our (nearly empty) glasses and putting heart and soul into having a great time. Yes, auditors certainly do have soul.

REFERENCES

Basu, D. (2008) *AudIT to BenefIT*. BCS, The Chartered Institute for IT. Available from www.bcs.org/content/conWebDoc/18596 [accessed 18 November 2015].

Cabinet Office (2014) *Security policy framework*. Gov.UK. Available from https://www.gov.uk/government/publications/security-policy-framework [accessed 30 November 2015].

Commission of Corporate Governance (2004) *The Belgian code on corporate governance*. Brussels: Corporate Governance Committee. Available from www.ecgi.org/codes/documents/bel_code_dec2004_en.pdf [accessed 19 November 2015].

Goo, J., Yim, M and Kim, D.J. (2013) A pathway to successful management of individual intention to security compliance: A role of organizational climate. In: *Proceedings of the 2013 46th Hawaii international conference on system sciences*. Washington, DC: IEEE Computer Society. 2,959–2,968. Available from https://www.computer.org/csdl/proceedings/hicss/2013/4892/00/4892c959.pdf [accessed 17 November 2015].

Lee, M. (2014) *The internet of everything: How smart buildings impact security*. Presented to IFSEC International 2014. IFSEC Global. Available from www.ifsecglobal.com/download-internet-everything-smart-buildings-impact-security/ [accessed 30 November 2015].

London Stock Exchange (2012) *Corporate governance for main market and AIM companies*. London: White Page Ltd. Available from www.londonstockexchange.com/companies-and-advisors/aim/publications/ documents/corpgov.pdf [accessed 19 November 2015].

Long, J. (2006) *No tech hacking: A guide to social engineering, dumpster diving, and shoulder surfing*. Rockland, MA: Syngress Publishing inc. and Elsevier inc.

National Institute of Standards and Technology (2006) *Information security handbook: A guide for managers*. Gaithersburg, MD: US Department of Commerce, NIST. Available from http://csrc.nist.gov/publications/nistpubs/800-100/ SP800-100-Mar07-2007.pdf [accessed 19 November 2015].

OWASP Foundation (2013) *The OWASP application security code of conduct for government bodies: Version 1.17*. Available from https://www.owasp.org/images/archive/d/ de/20150519104854!OWASP_Green_Book-Governmental_ Bodies.pdf [accessed 30 November 2015].

PCI Security Standards Council (2013) *Payment card industry (PCI) data security standard: Requirements and security assessment procedures. Version 3.0*. PCI Security Standards Council LLC. Available from https://www.pcisecuritystandards. org/documents/PCI_DSS_v3.pdf [accessed 30 November 2015].

Renaud, K. and Goucher, W. (2012) Email passwords: pushing on a latched door. *Computer Fraud & Security* 2012 (9), 16–19.

Renaud, K. and Goucher, W. (2014) The curious incidence of security breaches by knowledgeable employees and the pivotal role of a security culture. In: *Human Aspects of Information Security, Privacy and Trust*. Switzerland: Springer International Publishing. 361–372.

Sarens, G. and De Beelde, I. (2005) *Interaction between internal audit and different organisational parties: An analysis of expectations and perceptions*. No. 05/353. Belgium: Ghent University, Faculty of Economics and Business Administration.

INDEX